Harvard Business Review

on

GREENING YOUR BUSINESS PROFITABLY

The Harvard Business Review
Paperback series

If you need the best practices and ideas for the business challenges you face—but don't have time to find them—*Harvard Business Review* **paperbacks** are for you. Each book is a collection of HBR's inspiring and useful perspectives on a given management topic, all in one place.

The titles include:

Harvard Business Review

on

GREENING YOUR BUSINESS PROFITABLY

Harvard Business Review Press

Boston, Massachusetts

Library of Congress Cataloging-in-Publication Data

Harvard business review on greening your business profitably.
       p. cm.—(The Harvard business review paperback series)
   A collection of articles previously published in the Harvard business
review.
   ISBN 978-1-4221-6256-9 (alk. paper)
   1. Business enterprises—Environmental aspects.   2. Environmental
responsibility.   3. Management—Environmental aspects.   4. Social
responsibility of business.   I. Harvard business review.
   HD30.255.H372   2011
   658.4'083—dc22

                                                    2011000835

Contents

Harvard
Business
Review

on

GREENING
YOUR BUSINESS
PROFITABLY

Why Sustainability Is Now the Key Driver of Innovation

by Ram Nidumolu, C.K. Prahalad, and M.R. Rangaswami

THERE'S NO ALTERNATIVE TO sustainable development. Even so, many companies are convinced that the more environment-friendly they become, the more the effort will erode their competitiveness. They believe it will add to costs and will not deliver immediate financial benefits.

Talk long enough to CEOs, particularly in the United States or Europe, and their concerns will pour out: Making our operations sustainable and developing "green" products places us at a disadvantage vis-à-vis rivals in developing countries that don't face the same pressures. Suppliers can't provide green inputs or transparency; sustainable manufacturing will demand new equipment and processes; and customers will not pay more for eco-friendly products during a recession. That's why most executives treat the need to become sustainable as a corporate social responsibility, divorced from business objectives.

Not surprisingly, the fight to save the planet has turned into a pitched battle between governments and companies, between companies and consumer activists, and sometimes between consumer activists and governments. It resembles a three-legged race, in which you move forward with the two untied legs but the tied third leg holds you back. One solution, mooted by policy experts and environmental activists, is more and increasingly tougher regulation. They argue that voluntary action is unlikely to be enough. Another group suggests educating and organizing consumers so that they will force businesses to become sustainable. Although both legislation and education are necessary, they may not be able to solve the problem quickly or completely.

Executives behave as though they have to choose between the largely social benefits of developing sustainable products or processes and the financial costs of doing so. But that's simply not true. We've been studying the sustainability initiatives of 30 large corporations for some time. Our research shows that sustainability is a mother lode of organizational and technological innovations that yield both bottom-line and top-line returns. Becoming environment-friendly lowers costs because companies end up reducing the inputs they use. In addition, the process generates additional revenues from better products or enables companies to create new

Idea in Brief

When companies pursue sustainability, it's usually to demonstrate that they are socially responsible. They expect that the endeavor will add to their costs, deliver no immediate financial benefits, and quite possibly erode their competitiveness. Meanwhile, policy makers and activists argue that it will take tougher regulations and educated, organized consumers to force businesses to adopt sustainable practices. But, say the authors, the quest for sustainability can unearth a mother lode of organizational and technological innovations that yield both top-line and bottom-line returns. That quest has already begun to transform the competitive landscape, as companies redesign products,

technologies, processes, and business models. By equating sustainability with innovation today, enterprises can lay the groundwork that will put them in the lead when the recession ends. Nidumolu, Prahalad, and Rangaswami have found that companies on the journey to sustainability go through five distinct stages of change: (1) viewing compliance as opportunity; (2) making value chains sustainable; (3) designing sustainable products and services; (4) developing new business models; and (5) creating next-practice platforms. The authors outline the challenges that each stage entails and the capabilities needed to tackle them.

businesses. In fact, because those are the goals of corporate innovation, we find that smart companies now treat sustainability as innovation's new frontier.

Indeed, the quest for sustainability is already starting to transform the competitive landscape, which will force companies to change the way they think about products, technologies, processes, and business models. The key to progress, particularly in times of economic crisis, is innovation. Just as some internet companies survived the bust in 2000 to challenge incumbents, so, too, will sustainable corporations emerge from today's recession to upset the status quo. By treating sustainability as a goal today, early movers will develop competencies that rivals will be hard-pressed to match. That competitive advantage will stand them in good stead, because sustainability will always be an integral part of development.

It isn't going to be easy. Enterprises that have started the journey, our study shows, go through five distinct stages of change. They face different challenges at each stage and must develop new capabilities to tackle them, as we will show in the following pages. Mapping the road ahead will save companies time—and that could be critical, because the clock is ticking.

Stage 1: Viewing Compliance as Opportunity

The first steps companies must take on the long march to sustainability usually arise from the law. Compliance is complicated: Environmental regulations vary by country, by state or region, and even by city. (In 2007 San Francisco banned supermarkets from using plastic bags at checkout; San Diego still hasn't.) In addition to legal standards, enterprises feel pressured to abide by voluntary codes—general ones, such as the Greenhouse Gas Protocol, and sector-specific ones, such as the Forest Stewardship Council code and the Electronic Product Environmental Assessment Tool—that nongovernmental agencies and industry groups have drawn up over the past two decades. These standards are more stringent than most countries' laws, particularly when they apply to cross-border trade.

It's tempting to adhere to the lowest environmental standards for as long as possible. However, it's smarter to comply with the most stringent rules, and to do so before they are enforced. This yields substantial first-mover advantages in terms of fostering innovation. For example, automobile manufacturers in the United States take two or three years to develop a new car model. If GM, Ford, or Chrysler had embraced the California Air Resources Board's fuel consumption and emissions standards when they were first proposed, in 2002, it would be two or three design cycles ahead of its rivals today—and poised to pull further ahead by 2016, when those guidelines will become the basis of U.S. law.

Enterprises that focus on meeting emerging norms gain more time to experiment with materials, technologies, and processes. For instance, in the early 1990s Hewlett-Packard realized that because lead is toxic, governments would one day ban lead solders. Over the following decade it experimented with alternatives, and by 2006 the company had created solders that are an amalgam of tin, silver, and copper, and even developed chemical agents to tackle the problems of oxidization and tarnishing during the soldering process. Thus HP was able to comply with the European Union's Restriction of Hazardous Substances Directive, which regulates the use of lead in electronics products, as soon as it took effect, in July 2006.

Contrary to popular perceptions, conforming to the gold standard globally actually saves companies money. When they comply with the least stringent standards, enterprises must manage component sourcing, production, and logistics separately for each market, because rules differ by country. However, HP, Cisco, and other companies that enforce a single norm at all their manufacturing facilities worldwide benefit from economies of scale and can optimize supply chain operations. The common norm must logically be the toughest.

Companies can turn antagonistic regulators into allies by leading the way. For instance, HP has helped shape many environmental regulations in Europe, and it uses the resulting brownie points to advantage when necessary. In 2001 the European Union told hardware manufacturers that after January 2006 they could not use hexavalent chromium—which increases the risk of cancer in anyone who comes in contact with it—as an anti-corrosion coating. Like its rivals, HP felt that the industry needed more time to develop an alternative. The company was able to persuade regulators to postpone the ban by one year so that it could complete trials on organic and trivalent chromium coatings. This saved it money, and HP used the time to transfer the technology to more than one vendor. The vendors competed to supply the new coatings, which helped reduce HP's costs.

Companies in the vanguard of compliance naturally spot business opportunities first. In 2002 HP learned that Europe's Waste Electrical and Electronic Equipment regulations would require hardware manufacturers to pay for the cost of recycling products in proportion to their sales. Calculating that the government-sponsored recycling arrangements were going to be expensive, HP teamed up with three electronics makers—Sony, Braun, and Electrolux—to create the private European Recycling Platform. In 2007 the platform, which works with more than 1,000 companies in 30 countries, recycled about 20% of the equipment covered by the WEEE Directive. Partly because of the scale of its operations, the platform's charges are about 55% lower than those of its rivals. Not only did HP save more than $100 million from 2003 to 2007, but it enhanced its reputation with consumers, policy makers, and the electronics industry by coming up with the idea.

Stage 2: Making Value Chains Sustainable

Once companies have learned to keep pace with regulation, they become more proactive about environmental issues. Many then focus on reducing the consumption of nonrenewable resources such as coal, petroleum, and natural gas along with renewable resources such as water and timber. The drive to be more efficient extends from manufacturing facilities and offices to the value chain. At this stage, corporations work with suppliers and retailers to develop eco-friendly raw materials and components and reduce waste. The initial aim is usually to create a better image, but most corporations end up reducing costs or creating new businesses as well. That's particularly helpful in difficult economic times, when corporations are desperate to boost profits.

Companies develop sustainable operations by analyzing each link in the value chain. First they make changes in obvious areas, such as supply chains, and then they move to less obvious suspects, such as returned products.

Supply Chains

Most large corporations induce suppliers to become environment-conscious by offering them incentives. For instance, responding to people's concerns about the destruction of rain forests and wetlands, multinational corporations such as Cargill and Unilever have invested in technology development and worked with farmers to develop sustainable practices in the cultivation of palm oil, soybeans, cacao, and other agricultural commodities. This has resulted in techniques to improve crop yields and seed production.

Some companies in the West have also started laying down the law. For example, in October 2008 Lee Scott, then Wal-Mart's CEO, gave more than 1,000 suppliers in China a directive: Reduce waste and emissions; cut packaging costs by 5% by 2013; and increase the energy efficiency of products supplied to Wal-Mart stores by 25% in three years' time. In like vein, Unilever has declared that by 2015 it will be purchasing palm oil and tea only from sustainable sources, and Staples intends that most of its paper-based products will come from sustainable-yield forests by 2010.

Tools such as enterprise carbon management, carbon and energy footprint analysis, and life-cycle assessment help companies identify the sources of waste in supply chains. Life-cycle assessment is particularly useful: It captures the environment-related inputs and outputs of entire value chains, from raw-materials supply through product use to returns. This has helped companies discover, for instance, that vendors consume as much as 80% of the energy, water, and other resources used by a supply chain, and that they must be a priority in the drive to create sustainable operations.

Operations
Central to building a sustainable supply chain are operational innovations that lead to greater energy efficiency and reduce companies' dependence on fossil fuels. Take the case of FedEx, which deploys a fleet of 700 aircraft and 44,000 motorized vehicles that consume 4 million gallons of fuel a day. Despite the global slowdown, the company is replacing old aircraft with Boeing 757s as part of its Fuel Sense program, although it will postpone ordering new ones until 2010. This will reduce the company's fuel consumption by 36% while increasing capacity by 20%. It is also introducing Boeing 777s, which will reduce fuel consumption by a further 18%. FedEx has developed a set of 30 software programs that help optimize aircraft schedules, flight routes, the amount of extra fuel on board, and so on. The company has set up 1.5-megawatt solar-energy systems at its distribution hubs in California and Cologne, Germany. It uses hybrid vans that are 42% more fuel efficient than conventional trucks and has replaced more than 25% of its fleet with smaller, more fuel-efficient vehicles. Following some other pioneers, FedEx recently turned its energy-saving expertise into a stand-alone consulting business that, it hopes, will become a profit center.

Workplaces

Partly because of environmental concerns, some corporations encourage employees to work from home. This leads to reductions in travel time, travel costs, and energy use. One-tenth of the corporations in our sample had from 21% to 50% of their employees telecommuting regularly. Of IBM's 320,000 employees, 25% telecommute, which leads to an annual savings of $700 million in real estate costs alone. AT&T estimates that it saves $550 million annually as a result of telecommuting. Productivity rises by 10% to 20%, and job satisfaction also increases when people telecommute up to three days a week. For example, at the health-care services provider McKesson, the group that reported the highest job satisfaction in 2007 consisted of 1,000 nurses who worked from home.

Returns

Concerns about cutting waste invariably spark companies' interest in product returns. In the United States, returns reduce corporate profitability by an average of about 4% a year. Instead of scrapping returned products, companies at this stage try to recapture some of the lost value by reusing them. Not only can this turn a cost center into a profitable business, but the change in attitude signals that the company is more concerned about preventing environmental damage and reducing waste than it is about cannibalizing sales.

Cisco, for example, had traditionally regarded the used equipment it received as scrap and recycled it at a cost of about $8 million a year. Four years ago it tried to

Sustainability challenges, competencies, and opportunities

Stage 1 Viewing compliance as opportunity	Stage 2 Making value chains sustainable	Stage 3 Designing sustainable products and services	Stage 4 Developing new business models	Stage 5 Creating next-practice platforms
Central challenge To ensure that compliance with norms becomes an opportunity for innovation.	**Central challenge** To increase efficiencies throughout the value chain.	**Central challenge** To develop sustainable offerings or redesign existing ones to become eco-friendly.	**Central challenge** To find novel ways of delivering and capturing value, which will change the basis of competition.	**Central challenge** To question through the sustainability lens the dominant logic behind business today.
Competencies needed • The ability to anticipate and shape regulations. • The skill to work with other companies, including rivals, to implement creative solutions.	**Competencies needed** • Expertise in techniques such as carbon management and life-cycle assessment. • The ability to redesign operations to use less energy and water, produce fewer emissions, and generate less waste.	**Competencies needed** • The skills to know which products or services are most unfriendly to the environment. • The ability to generate real public support for sustainable offerings and not be considered as "greenwashing."	**Competencies needed** • The capacity to understand what consumers want and to figure out different ways to meet those demands. • The ability to understand how partners can enhance the value of offerings.	**Competencies required** • Knowledge of how renewable and nonrenewable resources affect business ecosystems and industries. • The expertise to synthesize business models, technologies, and regulations in different industries.
Innovation opportunity • Using compliance to induce the company and its partners to experiment with sustainable technologies, materials, and processes.	**Innovation opportunities** • Developing sustainable sources of raw materials and components. • Increasing the use of clean energy sources such as wind and solar power. • Finding innovative uses for returned products.	**Innovation opportunities** • Applying techniques such as biomimicry in product development. • Developing compact and eco-friendly packaging.	**Innovation opportunities** • Developing new delivery technologies that change value-chain relationships in significant ways. • Creating monetization models that relate to services rather than products. • Devising business models that combine digital and physical infrastructures.	**Innovation opportunities** • Building business platforms that will enable customers and suppliers to manage energy in radically different ways. • Developing products that won't need water in categories traditionally associated with it, such as cleaning products. • Designing technologies that will allow industries to use the energy produced as a by-product.

In Stage 3, the Central challenge description continues with: "The management know-how to scale both supplies of green materials and the manufacture of products."

find uses for the equipment, mainly because 80% of the returns were in working condition. A value-recovery team at Cisco identified internal customers that included its customer service organization, which supports warranty claims and service contracts, and the labs that provide technical support, training, and product demonstrations. In 2005 Cisco designated the recycling group as a business unit, set clear objectives for it, and drew up a notional P&L account. As a result, the reuse of equipment rose from 5% in 2004 to 45% in 2008, and Cisco's recycling costs fell by 40%. The unit has become a profit center that contributed $100 million to Cisco's bottom line in 2008.

When they create environment-friendly value chains, companies uncover the monetary benefits that energy efficiency and waste reduction can deliver. They also learn to build mechanisms that link sustainability initiatives to business results, as the Cisco example shows. As a result, environmental concerns take root within business units, allowing executives to tackle the next big challenge.

Stage 3: Designing Sustainable Products and Services

At this stage executives start waking up to the fact that a sizable number of consumers prefer eco-friendly offerings, and that their businesses can score over rivals by being the first to redesign existing products or develop new ones. In order to identify product innovation priorities, enterprises have to use competencies and tools they acquired at earlier stages of their evolution.

Companies are often startled to discover which products are unfriendly to the environment. When Procter & Gamble, for example, conducted life-cycle assessments to calculate the amount of energy needed to use its products, it found that detergents can make U.S. households energy guzzlers. They spend 3% of their annual electricity budgets to heat water for washing clothes. If they switched to cold-water washing, P&G reckoned, they would consume 80 billion fewer kilowatt-hours of electricity and emit 34 million fewer tons of carbon dioxide. That's why the company made the development of cold-water detergents a priority. In 2005 P&G launched Tide Coldwater in the United States and Ariel Cool Clean in Europe. The trend has caught on more in Europe than in the United States. By 2008, 21% of British households were washing in cold water, up from 2% in 2002; in Holland the number shot up from 5% to 52% of households. During the current recession P&G has continued to promote cold-water products, emphasizing their lower energy costs and compact packaging. If cold-water washing catches on worldwide, P&G will be able to cash in on the trend.

Likewise, Clorox was surprised to learn that household cleaning products are the second biggest environmental concern—after automobiles—in the United States. Its market research also showed that 15% of consumers treat health and sustainability as major criteria when making purchase decisions, and 25% to 35% take environmental benefits into consideration.

In 2008 Clorox became the first mainstream consumer products company to launch a line of nonsynthetic cleaning products. It spent three years and more than $20 million to develop the Green Works line, delaying the launch twice to ensure that all five original products performed as well as or better than conventional options in blind tests.

Clorox had to tackle several marketing issues before launching Green Works. It decided to charge a 15% to 25% premium over conventional cleaners to reflect the higher costs of raw materials. Green Works products are still cheaper than competing products, which carry a 25% to 50% markup over synthetic ones. After much discussion, the marketing team chose to put the Clorox logo on the Green Works line to signal that it performs as well as conventional Clorox products. The company persuaded the Sierra Club—a leading environmental group in the United States—to endorse Green Works. Although it sparked controversy among activists, this partnership strengthened Clorox's credentials, and in 2008 the company paid nearly $500,000 to the Sierra Club as its share of revenues from the line. Finally, Clorox struck special arrangements with retail chains such as Wal-Mart and Safeway to ensure that consumers could easily find Green Works products on shelves.

By the end of 2008 Green Works had grown the U.S. natural cleaners market by 100%, and Clorox enjoyed a 40% share of the $200 million market. Green Works sales weakened in the fourth quarter of 2008 because of the recession, but they rebounded in the first quarter of 2009. The tailwind has encouraged Clorox to launch more sustainable products: In January 2009 it introduced biodegradable cleaning wipes, and the following June it introduced nonsynthetic detergents, where it will run into rival P&G.

To design sustainable products, companies have to understand consumer concerns and carefully examine product life cycles. They must learn to combine marketing skills with their expertise in scaling up raw-materials supplies and distribution. As they move into markets that lie beyond their traditional expertise, they have to team up with nongovernmental organizations. Smart companies like P&G and Clorox, which have continued to invest in eco-friendly products despite the recession, look beyond the public-relations benefits to hone competencies that will enable them to dominate markets tomorrow.

Stage 4: Developing New Business Models

Most executives assume that creating a sustainable business model entails simply rethinking the customer value proposition and figuring out how to deliver a new one. However, successful models include novel ways of capturing revenues and delivering services in tandem with other companies. In 2008 FedEx came up with a novel business model by integrating the Kinko's chain of print shops that it had acquired in 2004 with its document-delivery business. Instead of shipping copies of a document from, say, Seattle to New York, FedEx now asks customers if they would like to electronically transfer the master copy to one of its offices in New York. It prints and binds the document at an outlet

A Few Simple Rules

SMART CORPORATIONS FOLLOW THESE simple rules in their effort to become sustainable.

Don't Start from the Present

If the starting point is the current approach to business, the view of the future is likely to be an optimistic extrapolation. It's better to start from the future. Once senior managers establish a consensus about the shape of things to come, they can fold that future into the present. They should ask: What are the milestones on the path to our desired future? What steps can we take today that will enable us to get there? How will we know that we are moving in that direction?

Ensure That Learning Precedes Investments

Top management's interest in sustainability sometimes leads to investments in projects without an understanding of how to execute them. Smart companies start small, learn fast, and scale rapidly. Each step is broken into three phases: experiments and pilots, debriefing and learning, and scaling. These companies benchmark, but the goal is to develop next practices—not merely mimic best practices.

Stay Wedded to the Goal While Constantly Adjusting Tactics

Smart executives accept that they will have to make many tactical adjustments along the way. A journey that takes

---

there and can deliver copies anywhere in the city the next morning. The customer gets more time to prepare the material, gains access to better-quality printing, and can choose from a wide range of document formats that Fed-Ex provides. The document travels most of the way electronically and only the last few miles in a truck. FedEx's costs shrink and its services become extremely eco-friendly.

companies through five stages—and lasts a decade or more— can't be completed without course corrections and major changes. Although directional consistency is important, tactical flexibility is critical.

Build Collaborative Capacity

Few innovations, be they to comply with regulations or to create a new line of products, can be developed in today's world unless companies form alliances with other businesses, nongovernmental organizations, and governments. Success often depends on executives' ability to create new mechanisms for developing products, distributing them, and sharing revenues.

Use a Global Presence to Experiment

Multinational corporations enjoy an advantage in that they can experiment overseas as well as at home. The governments of many developing countries have become concerned about the environment and are encouraging companies to introduce sustainable products and processes, especially for those at the bottom of the pyramid. It's easier for global enterprises to foster innovation in emerging markets, where there are fewer entrenched systems or traditional mind-sets to overcome.

Some companies have developed new models just by asking at different times what their business should be. That's what Waste Management, the $14 billion market leader in garbage disposal, did. Two years ago it estimated that some $9 billion worth of reusable materials might be found in the waste it carried to landfills each year. At about the same time, its customers, too, began to realize that they were throwing away money.

Waste Management set up a unit, Green Squad, to generate value from waste. For instance, Green Squad has partnered with Sony in the United States to collect electronic waste that used to end up in landfills. Instead of being just a waste-trucking company, Waste Management is showing customers both how to recover value from waste and how to reduce waste.

New technologies provide start-ups with the ability to challenge conventional wisdom. Calera, a California start-up, has developed technology to extract carbon dioxide from industrial emissions and bubble it through seawater to manufacture cement. The process mimics that used by coral, which builds shells and reefs from the calcium and magnesium in seawater. If successful, Calera's technology will solve two problems: Removing emissions from power plants and other polluting enterprises, and minimizing emissions during cement production. The company's first cement plant is located in the Monterey Bay area, near the Moss Landing power plant, which emits 3.5 million tons of carbon dioxide annually. The key question is whether Calera's cement will be strong enough when produced in large quantities to rival conventional Portland cement. The company is toying with a radical business model: It will give away cement to customers while charging polluters a fee for removing their emissions. Calera's future is hard to predict, but its technology may well upend an established industry and create a cleaner world.

Developing a new business model requires exploring alternatives to current ways of doing business as well as understanding how companies can meet customers' needs differently. Executives must learn to question existing models and to act entrepreneurially to develop new delivery mechanisms. As companies become more adept at this, the experience will lead them to the final stage of sustainable innovation, where the impact of a new product or process extends beyond a single market.

Stage 5: Creating Next-Practice Platforms

Next practices change existing paradigms. To develop innovations that lead to next practices, executives must question the implicit assumptions behind current practices. This is exactly what led to today's industrial and services economy. Somebody once asked: Can we create a carriage that moves without horses pulling it? Can we fly like birds? Can we dive like whales? By questioning the status quo, people and companies have changed it. In like vein, we must ask questions about scarce resources: Can we develop waterless detergents? Can we breed rice that grows without water? Can biodegradable packaging help seed the earth with plants and trees?

Sustainability can lead to interesting next-practice platforms. One is emerging at the intersection of the internet and energy management. Called the smart grid, it uses digital technology to manage power generation, transmission, and distribution from all types of sources along with consumer demand. The smart grid will lead to lower costs as well as the more efficient use of energy.

The concept has been around for years, but the huge investments going into it today will soon make it a reality. The grid will allow companies to optimize the energy use of computers, network devices, machinery, telephones, and building equipment, through meters, sensors, and applications. It will also enable the development of cross-industry platforms to manage the energy needs of cities, companies, buildings, and households. Technology vendors such as Cisco, HP, Dell, and IBM are already investing to develop these platforms, as are utilities like Duke Energy, SoCal Edison, and Florida Power & Light.

Two enterprisewide initiatives help companies become sustainable. One: When a company's top management team decides to focus on the problem, change happens quickly. For instance, in 2005 General Electric's CEO, Jeff Immelt, declared that the company would focus on tackling environmental issues. Since then every GE business has tried to move up the sustainability ladder, which has helped the conglomerate take the lead in several industries. Two: Recruiting and retaining the right kind of people is important. Recent research suggests that three-fourths of workforce entrants in the United States regard social responsibility and environmental commitment as important criteria in selecting employers. People who are happy about their employers' positions on those issues also enjoy working for them. Thus companies that try to become sustainable may well find it easier to hire and retain talent.

Leadership and talent are critical for developing a low-carbon economy. The current economic system has placed enormous pressure on the planet while catering to the needs of only about a quarter of the people on it, but over the next decade twice that number will become consumers and producers. Traditional approaches to business will collapse, and companies will have to develop innovative solutions. That will happen only when executives recognize a simple truth: Sustainability = Innovation.

RAM NIDUMOLU is the founder and CEO of InnovaStrat, a California-based firm that helps companies design and implement sustainability strategies. **C.K. PRAHALAD** was the Paul and Ruth McCracken Distinguished University Professor of Strategy at the University of Michigan's Ross School of Business. **M.R. RANGASWAMI** is the founder of the Corporate Eco Forum, a global organization of senior executives.

Originally published in September 2009. Reprint R0909E

Growing Green

Three Smart Paths to Developing Sustainable
Products
by Gregory Unruh and Richard Ettenson

SOON AFTER ITS LAUNCH, in 1987, Clorox's Brita water
filter seized a leadership position among pitcher filtra-
tion systems, and by 2002 it controlled 70% of the market. But over the next five years, as the market
contracted, Brita's share declined. Management's pa-
tience with the brand soon wore thin, and in May 2007
Clorox CEO Don Knauss told shareholders that Brita had
two years to improve or it would be sold off. "When I got
on board," Knauss remembers, "the question was, How
quickly can we sell this thing?" Then came a remarkable
turn: Brita recovered its momentum within months,
achieving double-digit growth and leading the brand
back with a vengeance.

How did its managers do it? By going green, as we'll
detail below.

That strategy wouldn't have been obvious 10 years
ago. But thanks to aggressive leadership by some of the

world's biggest companies—Wal-Mart, GE, and DuPont among them—green growth has risen to the top of the agenda for many businesses. From 2007 to 2009 eco-friendly product launches increased by more than 500%. A recent IBM survey found that two-thirds of executives see sustainability as a revenue driver, and half of them expect green initiatives to confer competitive advantage. This dramatic shift in corporate mindset and practices over the past decade reflects a growing awareness that environmental responsibility can be a platform for both growth and differentiation.

Nonetheless, the best approach to achieving green growth isn't always clear. This article is for executives who believe that developing green products makes sense for their organization and need to determine the best path forward. We will introduce and describe three broad strategies—*accentuate, acquire,* and *architect*—that companies can use to align their green goals with their capabilities. These strategies emerged from 10 in-depth case studies of consumer product and industrial companies that were moving into the green space; we validated the studies in discussions with dozens of senior and midlevel sustainability executives. The framework now plays a central role in the core executive MBA course offerings in sustainable business strategy and in the executive education programs at Thunderbird School of Global Management.

As we'll see, green product development brings with it unique cultural, operational, and execution challenges.

Idea in Brief

Most companies know that they need to be greening their offerings—if not to gain advantage, then simply to keep up. In this article the authors offer a framework for embarking on the green-product development process, introducing three broad strategies that companies can use to align their green goals and capabilities. An "accentuate" strategy involves evaluating products in the company's current portfolio and playing up or extending latent or existing green attributes (as Arm & Hammer did when it repositioned its 150-year-old baking soda as "the #1 environmentally sensible alternative for cleaning and deodorizing").

An "acquire" strategy involves buying someone else's green brand—an approach used effectively by L'Oreal when it acquired The Body Shop, Unilever when it acquired Ben & Jerry's, and Colgate-Palmolive when it acquired Tom's of Maine. Finally, companies with innovation expertise can use an "architect" strategy, building green products from scratch, as Clorox did when it developed its celebrated Green Works line. Unruh and Ettenson offer case studies, outline benefits and hazards, and describe the optimal organizational and competitive circumstances for each strategy.

Path #1: Accentuate

An accentuate strategy involves playing up existing or latent green attributes in your current portfolio. Of the three strategies, it's the most straightforward to craft and implement and thus is a good place to start.

Some companies find it easy to accentuate. For example, Church & Dwight's Arm & Hammer baking soda has attributes that were just waiting to be leveraged. As green competitors emerged, and as customers demanded more environmentally friendly choices, Arm

& Hammer's managers emphasized its green credentials, positioning the brand as "the #1 environmentally sensible alternative for cleaning and deodorizing" and "committed to the environment since 1846."

Other companies may have to work harder than Church & Dwight did, but they can still harvest low-hanging green fruit. Consider how Brita repositioned its water filters. A decade ago Brita's sales were siphoned off by the rising popularity of bottled water, which exploded into a billion-dollar business. But water bottlers attracted loud critics such as the World Wide Fund for Nature and Corporate Accountability International, which condemned them for clogging landfills with plastic and deceptively advertising their product as better tasting and healthier than tap water.

Brita's managers were quick to see an opportunity. Company research showed that replacing bottled water with Brita systems could potentially keep millions of bottles a year out of landfills. To capitalize on this benefit, the managers pursued an integrated cross-media communications strategy to tout Brita's green attributes, educate consumers about bottle waste, and encourage a switch to greener alternatives. As part of this strategy, the company launched FilterForGood, a website that invites visitors to pledge that they will reduce plastic waste by switching to reusable bottles. A device on the site graphically updates the tally of bottles saved. Brita's managers ensured that the media picked up on FilterForGood—for example, by arranging a partnership with NBC's television show *The Biggest Loser*. Within a year the company's water pitcher sales jumped a robust 23%, compared with just 2% for the category overall.

Brita's impressive success came in part because it did not overreach in its sustainability claims. Companies that decide to pursue an accentuate strategy would be wise to follow its lead. Activists and environmental experts will not hesitate to point out greenwashing or other undesirable corporate behavior when they see it. Consider the experience of Arm & Hammer. Promoting the environmentally friendly attributes of the product was easy, but the company overlooked a major liability: It used animal testing. Activists took to the blogosphere and called on customers to switch to the cruelty-free and equally green Bob's Red Mill baking soda. Although such complaints won't necessarily reach or resonate with all your customers, anticipating and heading off criticism will strengthen your overall greening efforts. Transparency in claims and authenticity in execution are important elements in the long-term success of any green strategy.

The broader your brand portfolio, of course, the more exposed you may be to activist and consumer backlash. Most companies lack a green heritage; their products were developed before sustainability was a concern. So they must carefully gauge how the rest of their portfolio will look by comparison with the accentuated product. Touting the green attributes of some products inevitably prompts the response "Great! But what about the rest of your offerings?" A big gulf between your green and nongreen products can undermine your legitimate sustainability claims.

Consider BP's troubled "Beyond Petroleum" rebranding effort. The company's Helios logo and the prominent solar panels on its service stations could not hide the fact that more than 90% of its revenues came from oil. *Fortune* highlighted the disparity when it wrote, "Here's a novel advertising strategy—pitch your least important product and ignore your most important one." To avoid negative commentary like this, make sure your strategy aligns with customers' perceptions.

Brita did that well. Its managers were careful in their initial communications not to claim that their brand was a "green product" made by a "green company." They recognized that Brita filter cartridges had to be replaced every few months and were not being recycled. Because the FilterForGood campaign was predicated on eliminating that kind of waste, the managers realized that they needed a recycling solution for the cartridges. They forged an approach in collaboration with Preserve, which manufactures products using recycled plastic, and with Whole Foods Market to provide a solution that was simple for customers and highly visible.

"The filter recycling program builds on the success of Brita's FilterForGood campaign," the company announced—and went on to share credit with its customers: "Now Brita users are making another positive impact by recycling Brita pitcher filters." By accentuating the product's green attributes and eliminating or mitigating its nongreen elements, Brita enhanced the credibility of its sustainability efforts.

Path #2: Acquire

If your portfolio has no obvious candidates for accentuation, a good alternative is to buy someone else's green brand. Many high-profile green acquisitions have been made since 2000, including The Body Shop by L'Oréal, Ben & Jerry's by Unilever, and Tom's of Maine by Colgate-Palmolive. In such deals the buyer's channel and distribution capabilities are often expected to substantially broaden the green brand's customer base. Within a year after Unilever acquired Ben & Jerry's, for example, sales had increased by 70% and Ben & Jerry's had displaced Häagen Dazs as the leading premium ice cream brand.

The prospect of such robust growth is of course appealing, but managers who seek another company's green assets should be mindful of two considerations: Culture clash and strategic fit. Any merger or acquisition can stumble when company cultures collide. In green acquisitions that have idealistic, iconoclastic founders and countercultural workforces, the problem is exacerbated. Consider Groupe Danone's takeover of Stonyfield Farm. When shareholders forced Stonyfield's founder, Gary Hirshberg, to sell, he spent two years compiling a list of conditions—including rules about worker protection and environmental restrictions on business operations—to ensure that the company's social mission would be preserved. It took another two years to close the deal. By contrast, Unilever got around some but not all of the "founder challenges" at Ben & Jerry's by completing what was in effect a hostile buyout of the brand. This approach caused many activists to cry foul and deprived Unilever of the wholehearted support of the ice cream maker's founders. Ben Cohen said, "Most of what had been the soul of Ben & Jerry's is not gonna be around anymore."

All acquisitions present myriad management challenges, so the problems of integrating an idiosyncratic green business may not seem like a big deal. But scrutiny by the green community may undermine the otherwise solid business benefits of the acquisition. Even if product sales go well, sharp questions will most likely arise about the new parent's green credentials. If the acquisition goes badly and sales tumble, not only is the value of the new asset diminished but—potentially even more damaging—the acquirer risks being accused of deliberately destroying a green competitor. Coke faced such criticism after it bought Planet Java coffee drinks and Mad River Traders teas and juices and then phased them out two years later.

An acquiring company's actions may have an adverse effect on the carefully crafted brand image of the acquisition. For example, when Danone's agreement with Stonyfield about employee protection ended, Danone sent out pink slips and met with hostile reactions in the press. Such criticism may have limited impact on the bottom line, but it can diminish the credibility of a company's green efforts.

Successful green brands are attractive targets because they have loyal customer bases and because they come with specialized knowledge about eco-friendly

Best Practices: Who Accentuates Well?

Supply chain: Nike requires that its leather suppliers not source from clear-cut Amazon forests.

Manufacturing: Frito-Lay installed solar panels on its SunChips factory.

Product: CSX markets rail as the most environmentally friendly option for moving freight.

Packaging: Sara Lee's modified packaging for Hillshire Farm has resulted in 900 fewer truck trips a year.

Marketing communications: Stihl points out that its trimmers and blowers have emission levels lower than those required by the EPA.

innovation and manufacturing, sustainable supply chain management, and green market development. Bill Morrissey, the vice president of environmental sustainability for Clorox, told us that Clorox had not only growth but also knowledge transfer in mind when it acquired Burt's Bees, which had two decades of leadership in the green product space.

Path #3: Architect

For companies with a history of innovation and substantial new-product-development assets, architecting green offerings—building them from scratch—becomes a possibility. Although architecting can be slower and more costly than accentuating or acquiring, it may be the best strategy for some companies, because it forces them to build valuable competencies. Toyota took this route when it developed the Prius. Although the company is currently addressing a raft of quality problems, the lessons of its architect strategy still stand. The Prius was not the first hybrid introduced in the U.S. market (the Honda Insight was), but it now dominates the fast-growing market for more-fuel-efficient cars. Toyota's bold move to create a green brand has paid handsome dividends. The Prius towers over the Insight, its closest competitor, in market share. Its dominance has so distracted consumers from rival brands that some Honda dealers complain of customers who walk into their showrooms and request a test-drive in the "Honda Prius." Toyota has also successfully transferred its hybrid expertise and green know-how to other brands in its portfolio. In 2005 the company became the first to establish green credentials in the luxury-car space when it produced a hybrid version of the Lexus. Over time, Toyota's luxury competitors were forced to follow suit. Mercedes-Benz and BMW recently introduced hybrid models to meet growing consumer demand and to establish their green credentials and capabilities, and Audi and Porsche will soon do the same.

Clorox, too, in developing its Green Works cleaning products, shows how companies with limited green expertise but substantial product development capabilities can architect a green brand. Green Works has received a lot of press, but the details of Clorox's strategy—which we studied from inside the company—are less well known. The line of household cleaners emerged from a small skunkworks in the Clorox Technical Center led by a handful of independent and dedicated scientists. In less

Best Practices: Who Acquires Well?

Negotiations: Colgate approached Tom's of Maine with trust and respect, viewing the deal as a partnership rather than a takeover.

Company independence: Unilever agreed to keep Ben & Jerry's separate from its U.S. ice cream business, with an independent board of directors.

Internal communications: Tom's of Maine assured employees that the acquisition would help Colgate innovate around sustainability principles.

External communications: A joint press release from Danone and Stonyfield highlighted the benefits "to both companies of two-way knowledge and talent transfer.

than a year company researchers established the benchmark definition and best practices for a "natural" cleaning product and proceeded to design a line of offerings that would deliver the efficacy customers demand. The big surprise came when the marketing team shopped the original five Green Works products (glass, surface, all-purpose, bathroom, and toilet-bowl cleaners) to major distributors, including Wal-Mart and Safeway. According to a Green Works manager, "The realistic part of our expectations was 'Hey, if we get three or four SKUs, we'll be pretty happy.'" To the team's delight, Wal-Mart wanted all five. Distributors across the board asked for the entire Green Works line and requested that the brand be extended into other categories.

The development of Green Works induced Clorox to accumulate a range of new competencies, including specialized knowledge about eco-conscious consumers' preferences and expertise in the supply chain for natural-product sourcing and procurement. Through its deepened relationships with Wal-Mart and other distributors, Clorox quickly doubled the size of the "green clean" market. Even niche brands such as Seventh Generation and Method benefited from its market development.

Making Green Growth Happen

With an understanding of the three paths to green growth, managers can begin to craft a strategy that suits their objectives and their business context. They should begin by evaluating each option: Is it feasible? Is it desirable? How would it be implemented?

Feasibility

In this step companies take stock of their assets along two dimensions: greenable attributes of their existing products and brands, and organizational green product and brand development capabilities. The first requires a careful review of opportunities to promote brands' green benefits. Of course, each product will have its own category-specific attributes, ranging from recyclability to energy efficiency to reduced toxicity. The Global Reporting Initiative's list of more than 70 sustainability performance indicators is an excellent resource for managers. It can help them to identify less obvious green features and benefits that are suited to an accentuate approach or to frame strategies and gauge capabilities required for an architect approach.

The second dimension involves appraising the company's green resources and capabilities. This may include a broad review of the processes and priorities for innovation and new-product development, supply chain management, the coordination of and collaboration among distributors, and even partnerships with environmental organizations.

Desirability

In this step, managers assess the strategic fit of each option with the company's objectives and the resources they can bring to bear on the green initiative. They need to consider speed to market and the investments, reputation, and competencies that the initiative will require. For example, an acquire strategy will deliver high speed to market for a company setting out with low green credentials and low to medium green capabilities—but it involves significant investment. A company choosing an architect strategy must have high green capabilities and medium to high green credentials—and be prepared for a low speed to market. Companies unwilling or unable to allocate major resources for green initiatives will find accentuation the most attractive way to enter green markets. For others, green growth may be part of an enterprisewide sustainability initiative to retool operations, shift the culture, and, ultimately, reposition the organization.

Implementation

This third step involves acting on all the factors that affect successful execution. As outlined in the sidebar

Analyzing Growth Options

To evaluate the fit of a given green product strategy, ask the following questions.

Accentuate

First steps What's our strategic goal?

- To leverage latent assets?

- Revitalize existing brands?

- Broaden appeal to green customers?

- Gain green credibility?

Are there potential green brands in our portfolio?
Do we have the resources and capabilities needed for this initiative?

Your portfolio How will this initiative affect the positioning of and resources for our existing brands?
Should our greened brand be a stand-alone or a strategic brand that puts a green halo on the business as a whole?

Your customers Which consumers in the category are looking for greener products?
Does our candidate brand have "permission" to enter the green space?
Can we enhance the value of green in the category?

Your competitors Are our competitors greening their existing products?
Can we differentiate our brand?
How can we exploit our competitors' green weaknesses?
How can we capture a "share of voice" in the category?

Red flags Do we have environmental skeletons in our current portfolio or business model?
Will our green claims be credible—or are we vulnerable to accusations of "greenwashing"?

Acquire

First steps What's our strategic goal?

- To capture customers?
- Bring in new green capabilities?
- Broaden access to mainstream customers?
- Gain green credibility?

Which companies would make attractive green acquisitions?
Do we have the resources and capabilities needed for this initiative?

Your portfolio How will this initiative affect the positioning of and resources for our existing brands?
Will the initiative provide new abilities that can be applied to other brands?
Should our acquired brand be a stand-alone or a strategic brand that puts a green halo on the business as a whole?

Your customers Can we sell the green brand to our current customers?
Will acquired customers view us as a credible steward of the brand?

Your competitors Is this the prototypical brand in the green niche?
How can we exploit our competitors' green weaknesses?
How can we prevent competitors from poaching our newly acquired customers?
Can we add green attributes to the new brand or emphasize existing attributes to increase competitiveness?

Red flags Do we have environmental skeletons in our current portfolio or business model?
Will our green claims be credible—or are we vulnerable to accusations of "greenwashing"?

(continued)

Analyzing Growth Options (continued)

Does the proposed acquisition have an iconic founder, a countercultural workforce, or some other aspect that might create culture clash? Can we preserve the integrity—"the magic"—of the acquired brand?

Architect

First steps What's our strategic goal?

- To create new green solutions?

- Develop unique competencies?

- Respond to new market needs?

- Gain green credibility?

Will an independent business unit be required?
Do we have the resources and capabilities needed for this initiative?

Your portfolio How will this initiative affect the positioning of and resources for our existing brands?
Will the initiative provide new abilities that can be applied to other brands?
What will be the relationship between the parent and the new line?

Your customers What innovations are consumers looking for in a greener alternative?
Does our parent brand have "permission" to enter the green space?
Will this initiative require us to develop a new brand?
Will we need to educate and develop the market and bring new customers into the category?

Your competitors Are we creating a new green category?
Can we differentiate our brand?
How can we exploit our competitors' green weaknesses?
Does the category already have entrenched competitors?

Red flags Do we have environmental skeletons in our current portfolio or business model?
Will our green claims be credible—or are we vulnerable to accusations of "greenwashing"?

"Analyzing Growth Options," companies must align their green strategy with their existing product portfolio and devote or develop the resources and capabilities needed to achieve their strategic goals. They must ensure that the strategy satisfies customers' expectations and, when possible, takes advantage of competitors' green weaknesses. Finally, they must address "red flag" issues that could undermine implementation.

———————

Whatever path you choose—accentuate, acquire, or architect—activists, customers, and the public won't see your green initiatives as independent of your other activities and offerings. Rather, they will view your efforts as part of the organization's overall approach. That means the companies that ultimately succeed in growing green will be distinguished by their commitment to corporatewide sustainability as well as the performance of their green products.

GREGORY UNRUH is a professor at Thunderbird School of Global Management and the author of *Earth, Inc.* (Harvard Business Review Press, 2010). **RICHARD ETTENSON** is an associate professor and a research fellow at Thunderbird School.

Originally published in June 2010. Reprint R1006G

How to Jump-Start the Clean-Tech Economy

by Mark W. Johnson and Josh Suskewicz

WHAT WILL IT TAKE to transition from a fossil-fuel economy to a "clean-tech" economy powered by renewable energy? Silicon Valley is teeming with new projects in this field, and bold policy proposals are flying around inside the Beltway. The Obama administration has pledged more than $100 billion for sustainable technologies; China plans to spend $200 billion, and the G-20 industrialized nations some $400 billion. Venture capitalists around the world have pumped in excess of $20 billion into clean-tech companies since 2005.

So far, the bulk of investment has been in companies using conventional business models in an effort to fit clean technologies into existing systems. Sadly, history shows that this rarely works. Start-ups predictably struggle when competing head-on against incumbents in established markets. Disruptive market forces could over many years enable clean technologies to supplant

41

fossil fuels the way the PC replaced the mainframe. (See the sidebar "An Evolutionary Approach to Clean-Tech Adoption.") But we won't have to wait that long if we can deliberately effect a wholesale shift in our energy infrastructure.

To be sure, this is an ambitious goal that requires thinking on a grand scale. The key, we believe, is to understand that in a major infrastructural shift, technologies don't replace other technologies. Rather, systems replace systems.

Edison's Insight

Thomas Edison grasped the systemic nature of technological transformation a century ago, when he introduced the electric lightbulb. He realized that the technology he envisioned—no matter how innovative—couldn't by itself sweep aside the kerosene-based lighting industry. Instead of asking how he could solve the technical problem of inventing a lightbulb, Edison asked how he could get consumers to switch from kerosene to electricity. He understood that despite the many advantages of electric light, it would replace kerosene only if it had its own, economically competitive network.

So, while scores of people worldwide worked on inventing a lightbulb, Edison conceived a fully operational system. His technical platform included generators, meters, transmission lines, and substations, and he mapped out both how they would interact technically and how they would combine in a profitable business.

Idea in Brief

Billions of dollars worldwide are pumped into the search for clean technology and renewable energy. So far, however, most investment has been in companies that are using conventional business models to fit new technologies into existing systems. A far better approach, say Johnson and Suskewicz, is to create whole new systems. The authors propose a framework for thinking about clean tech that consists of four interdependent components: an enabling technology, an innovative business model, a careful market-adoption strategy, and a favorable government policy. Two recent experiments show how this framework can be applied: Better Place, founded by the software executive Shai Agassi, has a network of battery-recharging and -switching stations to support its electric cars and a business model based on selling electricity (miles) rather than vehicles. It has a foothold market in Israel, where gas-powered cars are taxed far higher than electric ones. Masdar City, now under construction in Abu Dhabi, will be a carbon-neutral incubator of clean technologies, supported by the investment, manufacturing, strategy, and academic units of a government initiative. The city is itself a foothold market and will benefit from government subsidies, "free zone" status, and favorable regulations. Both enterprises provide hope for supplanting the oil-based economy.

It had been widely assumed, for instance, that low-resistance filaments were most appropriate for lightbulbs, because they minimized the amount of energy lost as heat. But Edison determined that to make electric light economically competitive with kerosene lamps, he would have to limit the amount of costly copper used in transmission. Thus he'd need a high enough voltage to maintain current within a narrow wire—which meant a high-resistance filament in the lightbulb itself. Edison's search for a lamp filament "was conditioned by cost analyses," the science historian Thomas Hughes wrote in the journal *Technology and Culture*. "In his notebooks pages of economic calculation are mixed with pages reporting experimental data, and among these one encounters reasoned explication and hypothesis formulation based on science—the web is seamless. His originality and impact lie . . . in this synthesis."

Edison tested his concept in a pilot project at his Menlo Park facility and then launched it commercially on a small scale in Lower Manhattan, a favorable foothold market because the buildings were close together and filled with potentially enthusiastic customers: Wall Street firms that were eager to be on the technological cutting edge and that had employees who worked long into the night. It was not coincidental that he was demonstrating his system to the very people who could fund its expansion. He also used his public standing to acquire regulatory support—for example, to get the needed permits despite opposition from the lamplighters' union.

Others had designed decent lightbulbs, but without coherent commercial systems their inventions were for naught. We should be looking for the Thomas Edisons of clean tech.

A Transformation Framework

Many of the difficulties of clean-tech adoption can be traced to the fundamental error of focusing on parts rather than on the whole. Like Edison's, our framework for thinking about new systems consists of four interdependent and mutually reinforcing components: an enabling technology, an innovative business model, a careful market-adoption strategy, and a favorable government policy. The clean-tech discourse has given far too little attention to the importance of business models and market adoption and even less to coordinating all four components into a coherent whole. Let's look at each of the four in turn.

An Enabling Technology
Systemic shifts are often instigated by the emergence of new technologies. The invention of the steam engine catalyzed the era of the railroad; the creation of the microprocessor launched the information age. But the real impact of these technologies was felt only after systems had evolved around them. The invention of the internal combustion engine gave rise to the automobile, but it was Henry Ford's production process and the construction of roads, gas stations, and so on that ushered in the automobile age, dooming the horse and carriage. As Edison understood, for such advances to become viable, they must belong to complex, interdependent systems whose components work together in specialized ways. Edison didn't try to plug his lightbulb into the kerosene system, or even to adapt it to the contemporary method of electricity generation, in which each location relied on its own power source. He knew that he needed to envision an alternative system, build it out of both old and new technologies, and properly integrate it from the ground up.

An Innovative Business Model

As we've written in these pages and elsewhere, successful commercialization depends on combining an offering that solves a real customer problem with a business model whereby the company can deliver that offering at a profit. The business model consists of the customer value proposition, the profit formula, and the key resources and processes the company must combine to deliver the offering. The unique way in which these elements are integrated to create value for both the customer and the company is the essence of competitive advantage. (For a more complete description of the business model, see Mark W. Johnson, Clayton M. Christensen, and Henning Kagermann, "Reinventing Your Business Model," HBR December 2008.)

New technological paradigms require business models designed specifically for them. Consider Google: Countless dot-coms attempted to fashion new businesses on the internet, but many of them simply replicated traditional media business models, such as those built on display advertising, and, of course, many of them had no business model. Google, however, paired its advanced search technology with a fundamentally different business model—advertiser-paid search—and became one of the fastest-growing and most profitable companies in the world.

Innovative business models can have a devastating effect on incumbents. The oil and automotive business models, for instance, built as they are around fuel, parts, and maintenance for the complex internal combustion engine, could be undermined by a new model that takes

An Evolutionary Approach to Clean-Tech Adoption

COMPETING HEAD-ON WITH fossil-fuel-based energy is exceptionally difficult. A century of investment and innovation has yielded a comprehensive network of energy production and distribution that powers our homes, cars, and factories more conveniently, efficiently, and cost-effectively than anything else right now. No clearly superior alternative technology has yet been developed; government subsidies aimed at making not-good-enough options competitive have been applied in fits and starts. In any event, no alternative will be viable over time if it can succeed only on an artificially created playing field maintained by permanent subsidies.

Not-good-enough technologies take root in markets all the time; the personal computer couldn't begin to substitute for mini and mainframe computers when it was introduced. But as improvements evolved and were tested in the less-demanding home market, PCs eventually became a better alternative in the mainstream business market.

Some clean technologies are following a similar path, starting out as small, basic applications—such as neighborhood electric vehicles in developed countries and off-the-grid solar power installations in the developing world—that may improve and become more competitive in wider markets. We applaud all these efforts. They are certainly smarter than simply throwing large sums of money at the technology of the month.

advantage of simpler, streamlined electric engines. The utility industry's volume-based profit formula—the more power consumed, the higher the profit—may well fall apart as competitors devise ways to capitalize on the smart grid's ability to make power distribution dramatically more efficient.

A Careful Market-Adoption Strategy

It is in a relatively simple and isolated business environment that key assumptions about integrating the technologies and the business model will be tested, adjustments to the system will be made, and concepts will be demonstrated to skeptical but crucial stakeholders. Clean-tech systems, like the systems they're intended to replace, will be complicated; how best to integrate their parts won't be clear at the outset. Edison ran his grid on direct current, going to great (and futile) lengths to persuade the public that alternating current (which could be transmitted over long distances far more easily, using transformers) was unsafe. Even he, the system's inventor, was unable to see how all the parts would eventually fit together.

The most practical and effective course in situations of high ambiguity is to take an emergent approach— that is, to make your best predictions about what will work and then focus on finding creative, quick, and inexpensive ways to test the assumptions underlying those predictions. This is good advice for new ventures in general, and it applies to systemic transformations as well, even though they often require big investments just to get started. The aim should be to make the least possible investment in the smallest possible experiments to preserve the minimum scale needed to demonstrate the concept.

Accordingly, nascent clean-tech offerings have to incubate outside demanding, competitive markets—in foothold markets, where the value proposition offered by even early-stage technologies and business models is so great that customers are willing to overlook their shortcomings.

A Favorable Government Policy

Governments have long been central in advancing the development of next-generation technologies. But they shouldn't support market-ready technologies unless it's clear that they can be delivered profitably. Otherwise, situations like the corn ethanol bubble of the past few years will be all too common. Government support is most effective when it's directed not just at nascent technologies but also at nascent business models.

In addition to funding new models, policy makers must amend regulations that inhibit their development—such as those against driving electric vehicles in certain neighborhoods. And because it's impossible to predict which new technologies will win out, policy makers should use limited regulatory experiments to generate political momentum.

That's the approach officials took in Stockholm in their efforts to alleviate traffic congestion. Previously, certain crowded cities had tried to reduce traffic and pollution by instituting variable taxes on cars entering busy districts during peak times. The taxes were highly controversial, so it's not surprising that before Stockholm instituted a congestion-pricing tax, some 80% of its residents told pollsters they disapproved of the idea.

In 2006 the city government ran a small-scale seven-month trial in one neighborhood, during which officials measured traffic and pollution levels and tested various taxation schemes. The residents of the district were surprised by the effect the program had on their daily lives: Their streets were less busy, it was easier to get places on time, and the air was noticeably fresher. Data backed up these observations, and positive reports about the pilot program abounded. Public opinion flipped, and congestion pricing for the whole city passed in a referendum by 52% to 45%. Since being fully deployed, the program has cut traffic by as much as 50% and air pollution by 14%.

Although it may be natural to think that systemic transitions start with a technology that gives rise to an innovative business model, or that government must step in last, the four components of the framework needn't be conceived in any particular order. But whatever way the process unfolds, the first step should be to envision a system that integrates all four. Then the system's viability should be tested, refined, and demonstrated in the real world.

Systemic transformation is hard. It's the biggest of big bets, involving many interdependencies and more than a little luck. So it's not surprising that there aren't very many examples of it and that those that exist are easy to criticize. But focusing only on the risks and the shortcomings of individual attempts will blind us to the lessons we can learn from pioneering efforts to create an alternative to the carbon economy. That's why we went to investigate two of them firsthand: Better Place, the much-publicized company Shai Agassi launched to create a viable electric-automobile network, and Masdar, the organization set up by the government of Abu

Dhabi to, among other things, build a city run entirely on clean technologies. To our knowledge, no one in the world is doing any better at taking a systemic approach.

Getting to a Better Place

Many readers will be familiar with Better Place. But studying it through a systemic lens, as we did in a series of executive interviews and a visit to pilot locations outside Tel Aviv, offers fresh insight. In 2005 Agassi was a top executive at SAP when he asked himself a daring question: How could he get an entire country, such as his native Israel, off oil? The answer led him to leave his perch atop the software world and become a clean-tech entrepreneur. Throughout his career Agassi had built software systems. He immediately realized that the oil dilemma was a systemic problem, and that the electric car was the key to displacing oil. But electric vehicles had been around since the nineteenth century and had never been able to compete with the convenience and relatively lower cost of gasoline-powered cars. Drivers expected to be able to travel hundreds of miles before needing to refuel—and to refuel quickly.

Technology

The battery is the primary impediment to electric transport. Today, batteries that can take a car as far as a tank of gas can are too big, heavy, expensive, and slow to recharge. But instead of focusing on how to make batteries work in the existing system, Agassi asked what new system would be needed to make them as convenient, effective, and affordable as gasoline.

He realized that divorcing the battery from the car would overcome many of the technological constraints. The Chevy Volt, which will go 40 miles between charges, uses only 50% of its battery capacity to preserve the 10-year life span of its fully warranted battery. If a company were to sell cars but retain ownership of their batteries, it would be able to squeeze more energy from each charge. Better Place's battery can go 100 miles between charges, because the company need not provide a full 10-year warranty.

But merely improving the battery doesn't address the convenience problem—that requires an entirely new technological system. Better Place's solution: an extensive network of easy-to-use charge spots where people can park near their homes and workplaces; automated switching stations that rapidly replace depleted batteries with fully charged ones; and a proprietary software system called AutOS that tracks battery life and directs users to charge spots or switching stations well before their batteries run out of juice.

Better Place's network is designed to make driving electric cars as easy as possible. It is also designed to overcome a subtler but equally significant hurdle to electric-car adoption: grid capacity. Critics of electric cars have long pointed out that if all commuters plugged in their cars at the end of the workday, the grid would be overtaxed. Better Place is preempting this problem: AutOS will monitor and manage when each car draws electricity, rather than automatically recharging it as soon as it's plugged in. Thus the company can engineer its overall power draw to occur when power is cheapest and stabilize the grid during times of peak demand. This capability—known as demand management—is enormously attractive to utilities, because it helps them balance their loads.

Business Model

As this solution was taking shape, Agassi sought the advice of President Bill Clinton, who pointed out that the electric car needed to compete not just for new-car buyers but for the far larger pool of used-car buyers. Clinton wondered if Agassi could lower the cost of the cars enough to preempt all gasoline alternatives. Could he, say, make the cars free?

Separating ownership of the $10,000 battery from ownership of the car could lower the car's cost substantially but not eliminate it. What would make it worth a company's while to give cars away? A new business model began to take shape: Agassi would sell electricity—miles—rather than cars.

This, he realized, is essentially what cell phone carriers do: They build the network and heavily subsidize the hardware—the phones—while customers pay for minutes of talk time. Better Place would peg the price of miles to that of gas, using the margin between the cost of gas and the much lower cost of electricity to provide rebates that would make electric vehicles significantly cheaper than comparable gas-fueled cars. In fact, the company could sell electric miles the way cell phone carriers sell minutes—with a range of plans, from pay-as-you-go to fixed-price contracts.

Market

Agassi needed to find a foothold market in which enough cars could be sold fast enough to make the network pay off. It had to be a contained setting to make comprehensive battery recharging and swapping relatively easy to provide.

Early on he had shared his ideas with Shimon Peres, then the vice premier of Israel, and won a champion. Given its small size, strategic interest in minimizing the political power of oil, and innovative, technology-focused economy, Israel was a natural fit for Better Place. Few of its residents drive more than 20 miles at a time, and cars seldom cross the border. "It's a perfect transportation island," Agassi likes to joke. "If your car has left the country, it's been stolen." Furthermore, 60% of new cars in Israel are bought by corporate customers for their employees. More than 50 companies in Israel have already signed up to convert portions of their fleets to the Better Place network.

Policy

Peres had already devised a fairly simple public-policy initiative to support the adoption of electric cars in Israel. New cars had been subject to a 50% import tax; the tax on gas-powered cars would rise to 72%, while electric vehicles would be charged only 10%. The tax on gas cars is slated to increase over time, speeding the shift to an all-electric fleet. In addition to creating these incentives,

Peres introduced Agassi to leading industrialists in Israel and Europe, one of whom became a critical partner in the venture: Carlos Ghosn, the CEO of Renault-Nissan.

That's policy on the national level; Better Place has learned that policy on the local level requires a lot more legwork. The company has had to approach municipalities one by one for permits to install charge spots. The hope is that a federal edict, or the credibility earned by a successful demonstration on the local level, will streamline this process.

As you read this, Better Place is blanketing Israel with charge spots. It has successfully tested an automated system in Japan that can swap out a spent battery for a new one in less than two minutes, and it is using conventional cars to test its GPS-based navigation software. Systemwide tests are set to begin in 2010, followed by a carefully staged rollout in 2011.

Better Place's destiny is far from clear, of course. Critics accuse Agassi of being too ambitious. And indeed there's a lot one could take issue with: For instance, people have pointed out that the switching stations require the batteries and battery placement in the cars to be highly standardized, which would restrict styling options for carmakers. One might also argue with the scale of the trial market. But what we do not take issue with is the coordinated approach. It's essential to work at the systemic level and to engage all four components of transformation from the beginning. Better Place is a compelling demonstration of how individual companies might go about effecting sweeping change.

Thinking on a Grand Scale

Suppose you had far more money, political control, and natural resources at your disposal than Agassi has. How might you approach clean-tech transformation? We went to Abu Dhabi to find out. One of the United Arab Emirates, Abu Dhabi sits on 9% of the world's oil. In 2006 its leadership launched the Masdar Initiative to focus on building a clean-tech sector, with the aim of diversifying the emirate's economy, offsetting its contributions to global warming, and making its growth more sustainable by leveraging its energy expertise and its abundant sunlight. It was an ambitious charter, and Masdar came up with a suitably ambitious plan: It would build a carbon-neutral city—the world's first—to incubate clean technologies. The project broke ground in February 2008.

Technology

Masdar City will use 100% renewable energy, much of it generated on-site. It will have no cars; instead, an all-electric, automated personal rapid transit system will ferry people around. A comprehensive network of vacuum tubes will carry all garbage to a central site, where it will be sorted to be reused, composted, or burned for energy.

The entire city will sit on concrete pillars seven meters off the ground, providing easily accessible space for basic infrastructure—sewers, electrical systems, and so forth. The streets and buildings are designed to funnel hot desert air upward, creating breezes to cool the city and concentrating heat in wind tunnels to be sent to the on-site desalinization system. This synergistic design will reduce the energy needed for air-conditioning and the production of fresh water. All in all, Masdar City will be a living laboratory for the integration of an impressive array of clean technologies.

Business Model

The Masdar Initiative consists of five distinct units, one of which is developing the city. An investment arm takes stakes in promising clean-tech start-ups and projects around the world, such as Solyndra, an innovative U.S.-based thin-film solar company, and London Array, a gigantic wind farm going up in the UK. An industries unit manufactures clean-tech equipment; its first solar-panel factory recently opened in Germany. A carbon strategies unit develops systems and solutions to deal with global-warming pollution and is working to reduce the carbon generated during oil extraction in Nigeria. The last unit is the world's first clean-tech-focused university: the MIT-affiliated Masdar Institute of Science and Technology, which enrolled its first 92 students, from 22 nations, this fall and will relocate from temporary quarters to its Masdar City site in 2010.

The units will share insights and provide mutual support; together, they promise considerable synergies. The companies Masdar invests in, for example, will have an inside track on bids to supply Masdar City, office space in the city, and access to the university's resources. "We will smooth out the technology development process," Dr. Tariq Ali, the vice president of research and industry

A Systemic Model

BETTER PLACE, SHAI AGASSI'S start-up electric-vehicle services company in Israel, aims to make electric transport as easy, reliable, and affordable as gas-powered cars.

Market Adoption

Israel, given its small size, desire to minimize dependence on oil, and innovative, technology-focused economy, was a natural foothold market in which enough cars could be sold fast enough to make the network pay off.

Technology

Automated switching stations can swap a depleted battery for a fully charged one in less time than it takes to fill a tank with gas.
Charge spots in business and residential areas will allow drivers to recharge while parked.
Proprietary software will monitor batteries and direct drivers to the nearest charge spot or switching station when levels are low.

Business Model

The batteries belong to Better Place, which sells miles (electricity), and makes its profit on the difference between the cost per mile for gas and the much lower cost of electricity.
Rebates from Better Place to electric-car buyers—like handset subsidies from cell phone carriers—will provide an incentive to switch away from gas.

Policy

Import tax in Israel has dropped to 10% for electric vehicles while rising to 72% for gas-powered cars.

---

relations at the Masdar Institute, told us. "Our units cover each stage of technology development, from basic research to implementation at scale."

But more significant in our view is what Masdar's parts add up to: a business model not so much for a company as for a country—an exercise in the deliberate creation of a clean-tech cluster. Michael Porter, of Harvard Business School, defines clusters as geographic concentrations of interconnected companies and institutions in a particular field that give competitive advantage to a region by exploiting its unique resources. Clusters feed on their own success, creating a virtuous cycle. As Masdar's university and other units get off the ground, they will attract more clean-tech companies to the city, increasing occupancy for the property development unit while providing easy access to top technologies and potential partners for the investment and industries arms. General Electric has already signed on as an anchor tenant. The first commercial occupants are set to move in by 2013, and the city expects within a decade to be home to Masdar's headquarters, the International Renewable Energy Agency, 1,500 clean-tech companies, and 40,000 permanent residents.

Market
Masdar is wisely taking a measured approach to implementation. It has installed a 10-megawatt solar power plant, and it is developing the city in modules, one neighborhood at a time; the first will be completed by the end of 2009. As each one is constructed, successes and mistakes will be carefully catalogued for reference in building the next. "We have learned a tremendous amount already," says Khaled Awad, the man in charge of developing the city. "The second neighborhood will cost significantly less than the first did and be built much quicker." As new technologies are deployed and

integrated, problems with implementation can be identified and fixed. This process is occurring irregularly around the world; Masdar is concentrating and accelerating it.

In effect, Masdar City is its own sheltered end market. Given a chance to mature with minimal barriers to implementation and adoption, clean-energy technologies and business models can become viable options both for building projects in the developing world and for retrofits in the developed world.

Policy

Clearly, as a government-owned entity, Masdar is in a position to enjoy advantages that can't be matched in countries with less political will, on a scale not possible in the private sector. Although independently managed, it was founded with $15 billion of government money. Abu Dhabi granted Masdar the land the city is being built on, made the city a "free zone" in which foreign companies can avoid otherwise onerous native-ownership requirements, and put in place policies to encourage entrepreneurship and innovation. In fact, Abu Dhabi views Masdar as its clean-energy-policy think tank and is working with it to craft favorable regulations.

It may be tempting to dismiss this model as impractical in more-liberal economies with more-democratic governments. But consider that the $100 billion President Obama and Congress are contemplating to promote clean tech in the United States is more than six times as much as what Abu Dhabi is investing in

Masdar. The U.S. government sets up free-trade zones in inner cities; it might also seed or encourage clean-tech clusters in the United States with some of that $100 billion. Given the imperative to work at a systemic level, the Masdar approach—delving deeply into a confined but comprehensive project—is more promising than shallow bets across a broad landscape.

Masdar's clean-tech ambitions are already having an effect beyond the walls of its construction site. In an effort to reach its goal of carbon neutrality, the development unit has asked suppliers to reduce their carbon footprints. This request has reverberated throughout the supply chain, motivating scores of companies in the Middle East and elsewhere to cut their carbon emissions and make their operations more sustainable.

Will Masdar be successful? Just as with Better Place, it's too early to say. In our view, the value of these enterprises lies as much in their demonstration of what might or might not work in the pursuit of a more sustainable economy as in their individual fortunes. By taking a systemic approach, identifying and wrestling with key assumptions, and discovering new ways to combine key elements into a whole, both companies are accelerating the development of viable clean technologies. And despite the scope of their efforts, they are actually reducing risks and costs while increasing efficiency. Their new systems are already taking physical shape. Will they become competitive enough to supplant significant parts of the oil-based economy? It's easy to be skeptical—but we think it's wiser to see them as models that the rest of the world should study.

MARK W. JOHNSON is the chairman and a cofounder of Innosight, a strategic innovation and investing company based in Boston. **JOSH SUSKEWICZ** is a senior consultant at Innosight.

Originally published in November 2009. Reprint R0911D

The Sustainability Imperative

by David A. Lubin and Daniel C. Esty

MOST EXECUTIVES KNOW THAT how they respond to the challenge of sustainability will profoundly affect the competitiveness—and perhaps even the survival—of their organizations. Yet most are flailing around, launching a hodgepodge of initiatives without any overarching vision or plan. That's not because they don't see sustainability as a strategic issue. Rather, it's because they think they're facing an unprecedented journey for which there is no road map.

But there *is* a road map. Our research into the forces that have shaped the competitive landscape in recent decades reveals that "business megatrends" have features and trajectories in common. Sustainability is an emerging megatrend, and thus its course is to some extent predictable. Understanding how firms won in prior megatrends can help executives craft the strategies and systems they'll need to gain advantage in this one.

The concept of megatrends is not new, of course. Businessman and author John Naisbitt popularized the term in his 1982 best seller of the same name, referring to incipient societal and economic shifts such as globalization, the rise of the information society, and the move from hierarchical organizations to networks.

Our focus is on business megatrends, which force fundamental and persistent shifts in how companies compete. Such transformations arise from technological innovation or from new ways of doing business, and many factors can launch or magnify the process of change. Business megatrends may emerge from or be accelerated by financial crises, shifts in the social realities that define the marketplace, or the threat of conflict over resources. The geopolitics of the Cold War, for example, drove the innovations that launched both the space race and rapid developments in the field of microelectronics—ultimately unleashing the information technology megatrend. Electrification, the rise of mass production, and globalization were also megatrends, as was the quality movement of the 1970s and 1980s. The common thread among them is that they presented inescapable strategic imperatives for corporate leaders.

Why do we think sustainability qualifies as an emerging megatrend? Over the past 10 years, environmental issues have steadily encroached on businesses' capacity to create value for customers, shareholders, and other stakeholders. Globalized workforces and supply chains have created environmental pressures and attendant business liabilities. The rise of new world powers, notably China and India, has intensified competition for natural resources (especially oil) and added a geopoliti-

Idea in Brief

Executives know that how they respond to the sustainability challenge will profoundly affect the competitiveness of their organizations—and perhaps even their survival. Yet most are struggling with how to integrate environmental efforts into their core business strategies. Many have a hodgepodge of green initiatives but no overarching vision or plan. The problem is not that they don't see sustainability as a strategic issue. Rather it's that they think they're facing an unprecedented challenge. But there is a roadmap, say authors David Lubin and Dan Esty. They argue that sustainability is a "megatrend," a transformative change in the competitive landscape—like the rise of the quality movement in the 1970s and IT in the 1980s and 1990s—whose course can be predicted. By understanding how firms won in prior megatrends, executives can craft the strategies and systems they'll need to gain advantage in this one. The key: Companies that pulled ahead in prior megatrends developed early capabilities in leadership, tools and assessment methods, strategy development, management integration, and reporting and communication.

cal dimension to sustainability. "Externalities" such as carbon dioxide emissions and water use are fast becoming material—meaning that investors consider them central to a firm's performance and stakeholders expect companies to share information about them.

These forces are magnified by escalating public and governmental concern about climate change, industrial pollution, food safety, and natural resource depletion, among other issues. Consumers in many countries are seeking out sustainable products and services or leaning on companies to improve the sustainability of traditional ones. Governments are interceding with unprecedented levels of new regulation—from the recent SEC ruling that climate risk is material to investors to the

Fueling the Megatrend

VENTURE INVESTING IN CLEAN tech reached a nearly $9 billion annual run rate in 2008 and shows signs of growing again after a slowdown in 2009. The flow of private-sector investment into the clean tech marketplace has been estimated at more than $200 billion a year—with fast growth not just in the United States and Europe but in China, India, and the developing world. And G20 governments have earmarked some $400 billion of their $2.6 trillion in stimulus funds for clean tech and sustainability programs.

EPA's mandate that greenhouse gases be regulated as a pollutant.

Further fueling this megatrend, thousands of companies are placing strategic bets on innovation in energy efficiency, renewable power, resource productivity, and pollution control. (See the sidebar "Fueling the Megatrend.") What this all adds up to is that managers can no longer afford to ignore sustainability as a central factor in their companies' long-term competitiveness.

Learning from the Past: Quality and IT

Megatrends require businesses to adapt and innovate or be swept aside. So what can businesses learn from previous megatrends? Consider the quality movement. The quality revolution was about innovation in the core set of tools and methods that companies used to manage much of what they do. Quality as a central element of strategy, rather than a tactical tool, smashed previous cost versus fitness-for-use barriers, which meant the table stakes were dramatically raised for all companies.

The information technology revolution was about tangible technology breakthroughs that fundamentally altered business capabilities and redefined how companies do much of what they do. Digital technologies deeply penetrated corporations in the 1980s and 1990s, and the trend accelerated as IT made its way into the daily lives of workers and consumers with the advent of desktop computing and the internet.

In both the IT and quality business megatrends—as in others we've studied—the market leaders evolved through four principal stages of value creation: First, they focused on reducing cost, risks, and waste and delivering proof-of-value. Second, they redesigned selected products, processes, or business functions to optimize their performance—in essence, progressing from doing old things in new ways to doing new things in new ways. Third, they drove revenue growth by integrating innovative approaches into their core strategies. Fourth, they differentiated their value propositions through new business models that used these innovations to enhance corporate culture, brand leadership, and other intangibles to secure durable competitive advantage.

The Quality Story

The economic downturn of the late 1970s, coupled with the 1979 oil shock, drove a dramatic shift in consumer preferences toward efficiency. Many industries were transformed, perhaps none more dramatically than the automotive sector. Of course, the seeds of change had been planted earlier. In the years after World War II,

Japan had rebuilt its industrial infrastructure on a model of high-volume, low-cost factories that mass-produced goods of questionable durability and quality. "Made in Japan" was not considered a brand asset. By the mid 1970s, however, Japanese government and business leaders had seized upon the ideas of Edwards Deming and others who stressed quality as a core value. This incremental, process-oriented approach to systematic improvement fit well with Japanese executives' views on how to drive change to compete effectively in the global market. Leading firms including Toyota and Honda embraced Total Quality Management (TQM) methods, fundamentally shifting their value propositions. Quality methods called into question the assumptions managers had relied on for decades, namely that high quality and affordability were mutually exclusive.

The focus on quality—initially adopted as a means of reducing defects—delivered a greater advantage to companies that took a holistic view and drove changes across their business operations. The famed Toyota Way applied quality methods to every stage of value creation from concept to customer—and ultimately to intangibles such as brand, reputation, and corporate culture. The reputational harm Toyota is experiencing thanks to the recent recalls underscores how important quality continues to be to the firm's central value proposition. Toyota's current troubles also highlight the need for firms to align core elements of strategy. In this case, the dissonance between its long-term quality strategy and a more recent topline growth strategy has seriously undermined Toyota's model for value creation.

Rey Moore, the former chief quality officer at Motorola, describes a similar evolutionary process at the communications giant. Like most firms, Motorola first used quality methods to improve fault and error detection and thus reduce cost, waste, and risk. As those methods proved valuable, the company began to redesign manufacturing processes and product development functions to proactively reduce risks of product failures, functional inadequacies, and other inefficiencies rather than simply detect them. As quality's potential business impact grew, Motorola developed Six Sigma methods and a standardized tool kit including items like Pareto charts and root-cause analysis models to take quality to scale. Eventually, quality became a defining attribute of Motorola's brand and culture and a source of competitive advantage. The same story unfolded at firms in all industry sectors as leading companies rode the quality wave to enhanced growth and profitability—delivering a clear quality premium for their shareholders.

The IT Story

When the recession of 1982 hit, pressure mounted at many companies to increase productivity, particularly by using emerging information technology innovations to drive cost savings. The early returns on these efforts were mixed. As with quality, skeptics described IT as a black hole into which firms poured money with little return. But some corporate leaders saw that the strategic application of IT could drive growth and provide decisive advantage. American Airlines, a classic example, captured more than 40% of all U.S. airline transactions thanks to its innovative Sabre reservations system.

A lesser known case is American Hospital Supply's deployment of a revolutionary online purchasing system, which allowed hospitals to order medical supplies electronically, reducing costs, time, and errors for both the company and its customers. Over the next decade, the Analytic Systems Automatic Purchasing system— better known as ASAP—transformed how AHS delivered value to its customers.

Building on its success improving efficiency and reducing inventory risk, the firm developed service innovations that enabled it to deliver any product from any manufacturer at any time from any desktop computer to any hospital supply room. In the process, AHS amassed an extensive product and price database that gave AHS a clear advantage over less nimble competitors. Finally, AHS used IT to evolve its business model. The company, which had been a single-source materials provider to its hospital clients, began taking over their inventory management and procurement processes. This IT-driven innovation established the AHS brand as the leader in its business with a competitive edge based originally on price and later on service and helped the company grow earnings from $42 million in 1974 to $237 million in 1984.

The IT and quality megatrends show us that firms seeking to gain advantage in sustainability will have to solve two problems simultaneously: formulating a vision for value creation and executing on it. In other words, they must rethink what they do in order to capture this evolving source of value; and they must recast how they operate, expanding their capacity to execute with new management structures, methods, executive roles, and processes tailored to sustainability's demands.

Getting the Vision Right

Just as winners in previous megatrends outperformed competitors by following a staged evolution in strategy, so too must companies hoping to lead (or even compete) in the emerging sustainability wave. The idea that mastering sustainability should follow a multistage approach is already apparent. In 2006, one of us (Esty) with coauthor Andrew Winston described such a strategy in *Green to Gold*. The framework has since been extended, notably by Ram Nidumolu, C.K. Prahalad, and M.R. Rangaswami in their article "Why Sustainability Is Now the Key Driver of Innovation" (HBR September 2009). As was the case in the IT and quality megatrends, pioneering companies in sustainability often start by focusing on risk and cost reduction and over time develop strategies for increasing value creation, ultimately including intangibles such as brand and culture. Let's examine the four stages of value creation.

Stage 1: Do Old Things in New Ways
Firms focus on outperforming competitors on regulatory compliance and environment-related cost and risk management. In doing so, they develop proof cases for the value of eco-efficiency. At its inception 30 years ago,

3M's Pollution Prevention Pays was just this kind of initiative. As of 2005, PPP had reduced 3M pollutants by more than 2.6 billion pounds and saved the company more than $1 billion. It also laid the foundation for the nearly completed Environmental Targets 2005–2010 program, which will reduce expenses related to energy usage, emissions, and waste by another 20%.

Stage 2: Do New Things in New Ways

Firms engage in widespread redesign of products, processes, and whole systems to optimize natural resource efficiencies and risk management across their value chains. DuPont's "zero waste" commitment, for instance, increased the company's prioritization of eco-efficiency across their operations. Its decision to shed businesses with big eco-footprints, such as carpets and nylon, was based on an analysis that the business and environmental risks would outweigh their potential contribution to future earnings.

Stage 3: Transform Core Business

As the vision expands further, sustainability innovations become the source of new revenues and growth. Dow's sweeping 2015 Sustainability Goals, designed to drive innovation across its many lines of business, yielded new products or technology breakthroughs in areas from solar roof shingles to hybrid batteries. The core business, which had traditionally relied on commodity chemicals, has shifted toward advanced materials and high-tech energy opportunities.

Capturing the eco-premium

Companies that excel in sustainability make shifts in five key areas, moving from tactical, ad hoc, and siloed approaches to strategic, systematic, and integrated ones.

Elevate leadership

Individual departmental leadership → C-Level leadership that links sustainability strategy with initiatives and outcomes, and develops shared goals in partnership with suppliers, customers, and other stakeholders

Systematize methods and models

Imprecise, inconsistently used tools that track discrete projects → Professionalized green business analysis through systematic use of specialized tools (e.g., scenario planning, risk modeling) and new certifications and standards

Align strategy and deployment

Unconnected tactical programs and initiatives → Megatrend-based initiatives aligned with core business strategies and embedded in operating plans

Integrate management

Siloed responsibility → Shared accountability through integrated objectives and performance evaluation

Systematize reporting and communication

Ad hoc reporting using nonstandardized tools → Sustainability scorecards that enable benchmarking, best practice comparisons, and consistent internal and external communication

Stage 4: New Business Model Creation and Differentiation

At the highest level, firms exploit the megatrend as a source of differentiation in business model, brand, employee engagement, and other intangibles, fundamentally repositioning the company and redefining its strategy for competitive advantage. GE's ecomagination initiative, poised to deliver $25 billion in revenues in 2010, enabled CEO Jeff Immelt not just to reposition the company as an energy and environmental solutions provider but to build a green aura into the GE brand.

Getting Execution Right

Gaining advantage in a megatrend is not just about vision—it's also about execution in five critical areas: leadership, methods, strategy, management, and reporting. In each area, companies must transition from tactical, ad hoc, and siloed approaches to strategic, systematic, and integrated ones.

Leadership

When CIOs first came on the scene, the role was ill-defined and narrowly focused. A limited set of problems was seen as suitable for IT solutions. Now CIOs play undisputed strategic roles with implications for all functions and business units. Strategic sustainability initiatives need similar C-level leadership. While many companies now have chief sustainability officers, the role varies tremendously from firm to firm. CEOs must make a commitment to institutionalizing this new executive position and allocating the necessary resources and responsibilities.

The CSO will be essential to moving companies through the sustainability stages. Like the CIO, a chief sustainability officer helps the CEO and executive team visualize goals and professionalize the process of aligning vision with business strategy. That means redefining performance expectations, specifying accountability, tracking results, and rewarding success. As best practices bubble up in individual units, the CSO is responsible for ensuring that they're disseminated widely and that the skills needed to execute are available.

Many firms are now accustomed to working with partners and suppliers in formulating their vision and goals, but a CSO must broaden and deepen those links as companies are increasingly held responsible for their entire value chain and product life cycle. Sustainability leadership must put a premium on developing shared goals with a broad set of stakeholders—customers, interest groups, and even competitors and adversaries. Coca-Cola, for instance, has worked intensively with its bottling partners to "light weight" its packaging, cutting greenhouse gas emissions and generating savings in the tens of millions of dollars. It has also made a commitment, in cooperation with its bottlers and the World Wildlife Fund, among other NGOs, to "water neutrality"—an initiative that will reduce its strategic risk and environmental impact by replenishing watersheds to the full extent of the water it extracts. In response to urging by Greenpeace, Coca-Cola announced in December 2009 that all its new vending machines and coolers would be HFC-free by 2015, reducing the equipment's greenhouse gas emissions by 99%.

Methods for Assessing Value

With a sustainability vision in place, the executive team must marshal specialized capabilities for weighing options and quantifying benefits and risks. Just as the quality and IT megatrends ushered in new skill sets and fresh perspectives, the sustainability megatrend will require firms to update traditional business tools—business-case analysis, trend spotting, scenario planning, risk modeling, and even cost accounting—to encompass the specialized requirements of environmental sustainability.

Most current methods that companies use to track or project sustainability impacts generate inconsistent, incomplete, and imprecise data. Recognizing that if they can't measure it, they can't manage it, companies are developing better means of gauging corporate-sustainability-related costs and benefits and of benchmarking performance. Fujitsu, for instance, employs a performance assessment scorecard—its "cost green index"—that assesses the potential cost, productivity, and environmental impacts of eco-efficiency initiatives across the firm.

Other companies are repurposing standardized tools and methods to bring a sustainability focus to all aspects of the business. For example, 3M, a longtime quality leader, is now applying lean Six Sigma methodologies originally aimed at improving operational efficiency and

Advice for First Movers

DON'T REST ON YOUR green laurels. As we have seen in other business megatrends, early leaders are not guaranteed enduring competitive advantage. Continued innovation is required to stay in front of the pack. Thus, even for those who manage a megatrend well and emerge at the top of a transformed market, the premium does not last indefinitely. For example, Wang led the world into office computing but failed to keep up as mainframes gave way to desktop computers. And while American Hospital Supply gained a substantial marketplace advantage by being an early mover in advanced information management in the health care sector, the competition eventually caught up and copied AHS's IT innovations. Nevertheless, the company's leadership in the IT wave allowed it to deliver superior value to its shareholders for a decade—not a bad ride.

product quality to driving direct reductions in energy use, waste, and greenhouse gas emissions. To meet aggressive five-year sustainability targets, its Six Sigma leadership group has trained 55,000 employees in how to use these methods. As sustainability-related methods and tools mature, we expect training programs and certifications not unlike certified IT roles or black and green belts in the quality domain to emerge.

Strategy Development

Once firms have a solid base of analytical data, they will be positioned to develop distinctive sustainability strategies. Many aspects of strategy development will remain internal, but companies will increasingly adopt open-source approaches that engage outsiders.

Perhaps more than any other company, Wal-Mart has pursued this approach. In 2006, then-CEO Lee Scott launched Sustainability 360, establishing explicit goals to purchase 100% renewable energy, create zero waste, slash greenhouse gas emissions, and sell "products that sustain our resources and the environment." To this end, Wal-Mart created a dozen Sustainable Value Networks, each comprising Wal-Mart team members, NGO experts, academics, government officials, and supplier representatives, all working under the direction of a Wal-Mart network captain. Each team focuses on a strategic issue targeted by the company's sustainability agenda—such as facilities, packaging, and logistics—and tries to develop new ways of doing business that support the company's sustainability goals. The payoffs are already showing up: One of the Sustainable Value Networks, tasked with fleet logistics, came up with a transportation strategy that improved efficiency by 38%, saving Wal-Mart more than $200 million annually and cutting its greenhouse gas emissions by 200,000 tons per year.

Management Integration

To capture the full benefits of the megatrend-driven strategy, firms must integrate sustainability objectives into day-to-day management. Leadership may come from headquarters, but responsibility for implementation lies in the field. Firms such as Dow have incorporated sustainability objectives into compensation models, reviews, and other management processes, including a requirement that all newly promoted business

Evidence of an Eco-Premium

RECENT ACADEMIC STUDIES OFFER new data correlating strong environmental or sustainability performance with superior financial returns. Notably, Julie Fox Gorte's analysis of a 2009 Mercer research survey examining several dozen studies found that firms with better social and environmental performance tend to have lower costs of capital associated with lower risk. The evidence is thus mounting that improved environmental risk management helps firms reduce volatility in shareholder value and earnings performance. We see this potential boost in shareholder value tied to the successful execution of sustainability strategy— what we call an eco-premium—as a further signal of the emerging megatrend's strength.

unit managers review their units' sustainability plans with senior management within 90 days.

Managing sustainability strategy requires systems support as well. While many firms have invested in technology to record and report environmental events such as spills and waste disposal, others have gone much further. Wayne Balta, head of Corporate Environmental Affairs at IBM, describes his company's environmental management system as the foundation for policy deployment, practice management, goal setting, decision making, and data capture. IBM uses the technology to embed environmental strategies into all areas of the business, from R&D to operations to end-of-life product disposal.

Reporting and Communication

As public scrutiny, governmental regulation, and customer expectations intensify, companies will need to build capabilities in sustainability reporting. For example, they will need to share information on their response to emerging environmental standards, such as the EPA's proposed greenhouse gas emissions reporting regulations, and on the financial impacts of the sustainability megatrend to employees, shareholders, and other stakeholders. Developing metrics that allow companies to measure benefits and understand costs is essential to adapting and refining their strategy, as well as communicating results. And Wall Street will increasingly demand evidence that sustainability investments are generating returns.

We see substantial room for improved sustainability communications, particularly among companies with a strong commitment to lead in this arena. Our firm has conducted evaluations of dozens of companies along 35 dimensions of sustainability management. When the assessments were based only on publicly available information and a company's external reporting, we got scores that were almost always lower, and often significantly so, than scores developed in consultation with the company and with full inside information.

We've found a few companies that are leading the way toward the sort of expanded sustainability reporting that we anticipate will become standard practice. Timberland's sustainability reports, for example, include numerous metrics on pollution and use of natural resources. The company has also broken new ground in providing product-level environmental-impact information to its customers with labeling that resembles the Nutrition Facts labels on food.

Building a Sustainability Performance System

By joining a vision of sustainability value creation (the "what we must do") with evolving execution capabilities (the "how we must do it"), firms develop what we call a sustainability performance system. Depending on their sophistication in both realms, and their desire to use sustainability as a competitive weapon, they'll fall into one of four categories:

Losers

As the sustainability megatrend accelerates, firms that have put in place only modest cost, risk, and waste initiatives and whose vision and strategies are vaguely conceived or disjointed will find it increasingly difficult to protect their position. It may be too early to see clear examples of firms that have lost their competitive position based on the failure to develop and execute sustainability strategies, but the casualties from other megatrends like quality and IT abound. GM's decline can clearly be traced to its earlier failure to understand how quality considerations would transform the auto industry. Likewise, Kodak's dominant position in photography eroded quickly as it missed or ignored the signals that digital technologies would displace film.

Defenders

Some firms may choose a "go slow" sustainability strategy for many reasons—the peculiarities of their industry sector or business processes, their environmental exposure, or other competitive considerations. Others will be content to make investments in the early-stage objectives of cost, risk, and waste management. This defensive posture can work, provided the gap between a go-slow company's market position and that of primary competitors does not grow too large and the company has execution capabilities commensurate with the complexity of its business. Maersk, the Danish shipping company, has focused its sustainability efforts on efficiency, slashing fuel costs and cutting carbon dioxide emissions through slow-speed shipping and other initiatives. As long as others in the shipping business do not pursue a more sweeping sustainability strategy, perhaps built on more-efficient ship design, Maersk should be able to hold its position. Indeed, many companies may find that their best option is to play defense on sustainability and not try to make this the issue on which they differentiate themselves in the marketplace.

Dreamers

When vision and ambition get too far ahead of the capacity to execute, companies face another set of issues. Those that seek first-mover advantages in the later stages of sustainability differentiation without having mapped out a clear strategy and mastered the fundamentals of execution may experience the same kinds of problems that plagued some aspiring pioneers in the quality and IT megatrends. For instance, the London Stock Exchange's vision of a paperless settlement system was a bold move and one that managers believed would catapult the organization ahead of its peers. Managers optimistically ballparked the cost at

£6 million and jumped in with both feet. By the time the exchange acknowledged that it lacked the management and technical capabilities to execute this leading-edge IT project, in 1993, the tab had shot past £400 million, with no end in sight.

Dreamers who try to ride the sustainability wave risk making sustainability promises they can't keep, inviting charges of greenwashing and the attendant reputational and financial harm. Some years ago, Ford Motor Company suffered from Bill Ford's attempts to green his business before his management team was ready. His unfulfilled commitments to improve SUV fuel economy and make Ford a leader in hybrid vehicles brought the

---

Making a sustainability winner

Companies seeking competitive advantage from sustainability must match innovative green product offerings and business models with strategic execution. Even those seeking to defend their position through eco-efficiency must climb the execution curve.

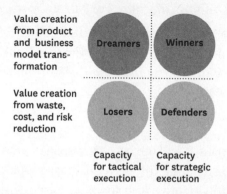

Value creation from product and business model transformation

Value creation from waste, cost, and risk reduction

Dreamers

Winners

Losers

Defenders

Capacity for tactical execution

Capacity for strategic execution

wrath of environmental groups. His successor, Alan Mullaly, has moved Ford forward with new models that feature advanced materials, smart systems, and high efficiency, enabling the automaker to withstand the current downturn better than domestic competitors and positioning Ford for success.

Winners

Although the sustainability landscape continues to shift, some early winners have emerged. GE's financial services business has lagged badly, but its ecomagination product line has generated tens of billions of dollars in revenues and positioned the company as a leader in rapidly growing market segments such as energy infrastructure and high-efficiency appliances, jet engines, and locomotives. The ecomagination marketing campaign has also had a halo effect, helping GE transform its reputation from environmental bad actor to sustainability front-runner. Similarly, Clorox's Greenworks line of eco-friendly cleaning products has reframed the public's perception of the company—and generated billions of dollars of sales. Clorox's acquisition of Burt's Bees, a leader in natural personal care products, further convinced environmental stakeholders that the company's shift in strategy was both sincere and significant.

Soon companies will have a clear sense of what it means to manage sustainability as a business megatrend. Best practices will emerge, and sustainability scorecards will allow companies to track cost and risk reduction as well as evaluate value-creation activities. As environmental data become richer and more accurate, companies will be able to chart their impacts in financial terms—making it easier for market analysts to identify the firms positioned to deliver an eco-premium. In this new world, the sustainability strategy imperative will be systematized and integrated into the day-to-day practices of firms of all sizes in all industries. Like the IT and quality megatrends, sustainability will touch every function, every business line, every employee. On the way to this future, firms with a clear vision and the execution capabilities to navigate the megatrend will come out ahead. Those that don't will be left by the wayside.

DAVID A. LUBIN is the chairman of the Sustainability Network, an Esty Environmental Partners service in partnership with IBM. DANIEL C. ESTY is the Hillhouse Professor of Environmental Law and Policy at Yale University and the chairman of Esty Environmental Partners.

Originally published in May 2010. Reprint R1005A

Strategy & Society

The Link Between Competitive Advantage
and Corporate Social Responsibility
by Michael E. Porter and Mark R. Kramer

GOVERNMENTS, ACTIVISTS, AND THE media have become adept at holding companies to account for the social consequences of their activities. Myriad organizations rank companies on the performance of their corporate social responsibility (CSR), and, despite sometimes questionable methodologies, these rankings attract considerable publicity. As a result, CSR has emerged as an inescapable priority for business leaders in every country.

Many companies have already done much to improve the social and environmental consequences of their activities, yet these efforts have not been nearly as productive as they could be—for two reasons. First, they pit business against society, when clearly the two are interdependent. Second, they pressure companies to think of corporate social responsibility in generic ways instead of in the way most appropriate to each firm's strategy.

The fact is, the prevailing approaches to CSR are so fragmented and so disconnected from business and strategy as to obscure many of the greatest opportunities for companies to benefit society. If, instead, corporations were to analyze their prospects for social responsibility using the same frameworks that guide their core business choices, they would discover that CSR can be much more than a cost, a constraint, or a charitable deed—it can be a source of opportunity, innovation, and competitive advantage.

In this article, we propose a new way to look at the relationship between business and society that does not treat corporate success and social welfare as a zero-sum game. We introduce a framework companies can use to identify all of the effects, both positive and negative, they have on society; determine which ones to address; and suggest effective ways to do so. When looked at strategically, corporate social responsibility can become a source of tremendous social progress, as the business applies its considerable resources, expertise, and insights to activities that benefit society.

The Emergence of Corporate Social Responsibility

Heightened corporate attention to CSR has not been entirely voluntary. Many companies awoke to it only after being surprised by public responses to issues they had not previously thought were part of their business responsibilities. Nike, for example, faced an extensive consumer boycott after the *New York Times* and other media outlets reported abusive labor practices at some of its Indonesian suppliers in the early 1990s. Shell Oil's

Idea in Brief

Many firms' corporate social responsibility (CSR) efforts are counterproductive, for two reasons: They pit business against society, when the two are actually interdependent. And they pressure companies to think of CSR in generic ways, instead of crafting social initiatives appropriate to their individual strategies.

CSR can be much more than just a cost, constraint, or charitable deed. Approached strategically, it generates opportunity, innovation, and competitive advantage for corporations—while solving pressing social problems.

How to practice strategic CSR? Porter and Kramer advise pioneering innovations in your offerings and operations that create distinctive value for your company *and* society. Take Toyota. The company's early response to public concern about auto emissions gave rise to the hybrid-engine Prius. The Prius has not only significantly reduced pollutants; it's given Toyota an enviable lead over rivals in hybrid technology.

decision to sink the *Brent Spar,* an obsolete oil rig, in the North Sea led to Greenpeace protests in 1995 and to international headlines. Pharmaceutical companies discovered that they were expected to respond to the AIDS pandemic in Africa even though it was far removed from their primary product lines and markets. Fast-food and packaged food companies are now being held responsible for obesity and poor nutrition.

Activist organizations of all kinds, both on the right and the left, have grown much more aggressive and effective in bringing public pressure to bear on corporations. Activists may target the most visible or successful companies merely to draw attention to an issue, even if those corporations actually have had little impact on the problem at hand. Nestlé, for example, the world's largest purveyor of bottled water, has become a major

Idea in Practice

To practice strategic CSR:

1. **Identify points of intersection between your company and society.**

- In what ways does your organization affect society? For example, do you provide safe working conditions and reasonable wages? Do your operations create environmental hazards?

- How does society affect your competitiveness? For instance, do countries where you operate protect intellectual property? Supply enough talented workers? Encourage outside investors?

2. **Select social issues to address.** Given your company's and society's impact on each other, how might you address social needs in ways that create shared value—a meaningful benefit for society that also adds to your company's bottom line?

   Example: By addressing the AIDS pandemic in Africa, a mining company such as Anglo American would not only improve the standard of living on that continent; it would also improve the productivity of the African labor force on which its success depends.

3. **Mount a small number of initiatives that generate large and distinctive benefits for society and your company.**

   Example: To enter the Indian market, Nestlé needed to establish local sources of milk

target in the global debate about access to fresh water, despite the fact that Nestlé's bottled water sales consume just 0.0008% of the world's fresh water supply. The inefficiency of agricultural irrigation, which uses 70% of the world's supply annually, is a far more pressing issue, but it offers no equally convenient multinational corporation to target.

Debates about CSR have moved all the way into corporate boardrooms. In 2005, 360 different CSR-related

from a large, diversified base of small farmers. It received government permission to build a dairy in the district of Moga. But in Moga, farmers were impoverished, failed crops led to a high death rate in calves, and lack of refrigeration prevented farmers from shipping milk or keeping it fresh.

Nestlé built refrigerated dairies as milk collection points in each Moga town and sent its trucks to the dairies to collect the milk. With the trucks went veterinarians, nutritionists, agronomists, and quality assurance experts. Farmers learned that milk quality hinged on adequate feed crop irrigation. With financing and technical assistance from Nestlé, farmers dug deep-bore wells. The consequent improved irrigation reduced calves' death rate 75%, increased milk production 50-fold, and allowed Nestlé to pay higher prices to farmers than those set by the government.

With steady revenues, farmers could now obtain credit. Moga's standard of living improved: More homes had electricity and telephones; more towns established primary, secondary, and high schools; and Moga had five times the number of doctors as neighboring regions. Meanwhile, Nestlé gained a stable supply of high quality commodities—without having to pay middlemen—and saw demand for its products increase in India.

shareholder resolutions were filed on issues ranging from labor conditions to global warming. Government regulation increasingly mandates social responsibility reporting. Pending legislation in the UK, for example, would require every publicly listed company to disclose ethical, social, and environmental risks in its annual report. These pressures clearly demonstrate the extent to which external stakeholders are seeking to hold companies accountable for social issues and highlight the potentially large financial risks for any firm whose conduct is deemed unacceptable.

While businesses have awakened to these risks, they are much less clear on what to do about them. In fact, the most common corporate response has been neither strategic nor operational but cosmetic: public relations and media campaigns, the centerpieces of which are often glossy CSR reports that showcase companies' social and environmental good deeds. Of the 250 largest multinational corporations, 64% published CSR reports in 2005, either within their annual report or, for most, in separate sustainability reports—supporting a new cottage industry of report writers.

Such publications rarely offer a coherent framework for CSR activities, let alone a strategic one. Instead, they aggregate anecdotes about uncoordinated initiatives to demonstrate a company's social sensitivity. What these reports leave out is often as telling as what they include. Reductions in pollution, waste, carbon emissions, or energy use, for example, may be documented for specific divisions or regions but not for the company as a whole. Philanthropic initiatives are typically described in terms of dollars or volunteer hours spent but almost never in terms of impact. Forward-looking commitments to reach explicit performance targets are even rarer.

This proliferation of CSR reports has been paralleled by growth in CSR ratings and rankings. While rigorous and reliable ratings might constructively influence corporate behavior, the existing cacophony of self-appointed scorekeepers does little more than add to the confusion. (See the sidebar "The Ratings Game.")

In an effort to move beyond this confusion, corporate leaders have turned for advice to a growing collection of increasingly sophisticated nonprofit organizations, consulting firms, and academic experts. A rich literature on CSR has emerged, though what practical guidance it offers corporate leaders is often unclear. Examining the primary schools of thought about CSR is an essential starting point in understanding why a new approach is needed to integrating social considerations more effectively into core business operations and strategy.

Four Prevailing Justifications for CSR

Broadly speaking, proponents of CSR have used four arguments to make their case: moral obligation, sustainability, license to operate, and reputation. The moral appeal—arguing that companies have a duty to be good citizens and to "do the right thing"—is prominent in the goal of Business for Social Responsibility, the leading nonprofit CSR business association in the United States. It asks that its members "achieve commercial success in ways that honor ethical values and respect people, communities, and the natural environment." Sustainability emphasizes environmental and community stewardship. An excellent definition was developed in the 1980s by Norwegian Prime Minister Gro Harlem Brundtland and used by the World Business Council for Sustainable Development: "Meeting the needs of the present without compromising the ability of future generations to meet their own needs." The notion of license

The Ratings Game

MEASURING AND PUBLICIZING SOCIAL performance is a potentially powerful way to influence corporate behavior—assuming that the ratings are consistently measured and accurately reflect corporate social impact. Unfortunately, neither condition holds true in the current profusion of CSR checklists.

The criteria used in the rankings vary widely. The Dow Jones Sustainability Index, for example, includes aspects of economic performance in its evaluation. It weights customer service almost 50% more heavily than corporate citizenship. The equally prominent FTSE4Good Index, by contrast, contains no measures of economic performance or customer service at all. Even when criteria happen to be the same, they are invariably weighted differently in the final scoring.

Beyond the choice of criteria and their weightings lies the even more perplexing question of how to judge whether the criteria have been met. Most media, nonprofits, and investment advisory organizations have too few resources to audit a universe of complicated global corporate activities. As a result, they tend to use

---

to operate derives from the fact that every company needs tacit or explicit permission from governments, communities, and numerous other stakeholders to do business. Finally, reputation is used by many companies to justify CSR initiatives on the grounds that they will improve a company's image, strengthen its brand, enliven morale, and even raise the value of its stock. These justifications have advanced thinking in the field, but none offers sufficient guidance for the difficult choices corporate leaders must make. Consider the practical limitations of each approach.

The CSR field remains strongly imbued with a moral imperative. In some areas, such as honesty in filing

measures for which data are readily and inexpensively available, even though they may not be good proxies for the social or environmental effects they are intended to reflect. The Dow Jones Sustainability Index, for example, uses the size of a company's board as a measure of community involvement, even though size and involvement may be entirely unrelated.

Finally, even if the measures chosen accurately reflect social impact, the data are frequently unreliable. Most ratings rely on surveys whose response rates are statistically insignificant, as well as on self-reported company data that have not been verified externally. Companies with the most to hide are the least likely to respond. The result is a jumble of largely meaningless rankings, allowing almost any company to boast that it meets some measure of social responsibility—and most do.

For a fuller discussion of the problem of CSR ratings, see Aaron Chatterji and David Levine, "Breaking Down the Wall of Codes: Evaluating Non-Financial Performance Measurement," *California Management Review*, Winter 2006.

---

financial statements and operating within the law, moral considerations are easy to understand and apply. It is the nature of moral obligations to be absolute mandates, however, while most corporate social choices involve balancing competing values, interests, and costs. Google's recent entry into China, for example, has created an irreconcilable conflict between its U.S. customers' abhorrence of censorship and the legal constraints imposed by the Chinese government. The moral calculus needed to weigh one social benefit against another, or against its financial costs, has yet to be developed. Moral principles do not tell a pharmaceutical company how to allocate its revenues among subsidizing care for the indigent today, developing cures for the future, and providing dividends to its investors.

The principle of sustainability appeals to enlightened self-interest, often invoking the so-called triple bottom line of economic, social, and environmental performance. In other words, companies should operate in ways that secure long-term economic performance by avoiding short-term behavior that is socially detrimental or environmentally wasteful. The principle works best for issues that coincide with a company's economic or regulatory interests. DuPont, for example, has saved over $2 billion from reductions in energy use since 1990. Changes to the materials McDonald's uses to wrap its food have reduced its solid waste by 30%. These were smart business decisions entirely apart from their environmental benefits. In other areas, however, the notion of sustainability can become so vague as to be meaningless. Transparency may be said to be more "sustainable" than corruption. Good employment practices are more "sustainable" than sweatshops. Philanthropy may contribute to the "sustainability" of a society. However true these assertions are, they offer little basis for balancing long-term objectives against the short-term costs they incur. The sustainability school raises questions about these trade-offs without offering a framework to answer them. Managers without a strategic understanding of CSR are prone to postpone these costs, which can lead to far greater costs when the company is later judged to have violated its social obligation.

The license-to-operate approach, by contrast, is far more pragmatic. It offers a concrete way for a business to identify social issues that matter to its stakeholders and make decisions about them. This approach also fosters constructive dialogue with regulators, the local citizenry, and activists—one reason, perhaps, that it is especially prevalent among companies that depend on government consent, such as those in mining and other highly regulated and extractive industries. That is also why the approach is common at companies that rely on the forbearance of their neighbors, such as those, like chemical manufacturing, whose operations are noxious or environmentally hazardous. By seeking to satisfy stakeholders, however, companies cede primary control of their CSR agendas to outsiders. Stakeholders' views are obviously important, but these groups can never fully understand a corporation's capabilities, competitive positioning, or the trade-offs it must make. Nor does the vehemence of a stakeholder group necessarily signify the importance of an issue—either to the company or to the world. A firm that views CSR as a way to placate pressure groups often finds that its approach devolves into a series of short-term defensive reactions—a never-ending public relations palliative with minimal value to society and no strategic benefit for the business.

Finally, the reputation argument seeks that strategic benefit but rarely finds it. Concerns about reputation, like license to operate, focus on satisfying external audiences. In consumer-oriented companies, it often leads to high-profile cause-related marketing campaigns.

In stigmatized industries, such as chemicals and energy, a company may instead pursue social responsibility initiatives as a form of insurance, in the hope that its reputation for social consciousness will temper public criticism in the event of a crisis. This rationale once again risks confusing public relations with social and business results.

A few corporations, such as Ben & Jerry's, Newman's Own, Patagonia, and the Body Shop, have distinguished themselves through an extraordinary long-term commitment to social responsibility. But even for these companies, the social impact achieved, much less the business benefit, is hard to determine. Studies of the effect of a company's social reputation on consumer purchasing preferences or on stock market performance have been inconclusive at best. As for the concept of CSR as insurance, the connection between the good deeds and consumer attitudes is so indirect as to be impossible to measure. Having no way to quantify the benefits of these investments puts such CSR programs on shaky ground, liable to be dislodged by a change of management or a swing in the business cycle.

All four schools of thought share the same weakness: They focus on the tension between business and society rather than on their interdependence. Each creates a generic rationale that is not tied to the strategy and operations of any specific company or the places in which it operates. Consequently, none of them is sufficient to help a company identify, prioritize, and address the social issues that matter most or the ones on which it can make the biggest impact. The result is oftentimes a hodgepodge of uncoordinated CSR and philanthropic activities disconnected from the company's strategy that neither make any meaningful social impact nor strengthen the firm's long-term competitiveness. Internally, CSR practices and initiatives are often isolated from operating units—and even separated from corporate philanthropy. Externally, the company's social impact becomes diffused among numerous unrelated efforts, each responding to a different stakeholder group or corporate pressure point.

The consequence of this fragmentation is a tremendous lost opportunity. The power of corporations to create social benefit is dissipated, and so is the potential of companies to take actions that would support both their communities and their business goals.

Integrating Business and Society

To advance CSR, we must root it in a broad understanding of the interrelationship between a corporation and society while at the same time anchoring it in the strategies and activities of specific companies. To say broadly that business and society need each other might seem like a cliché, but it is also the basic truth that will pull companies out of the muddle that their current corporate-responsibility thinking has created.

Successful corporations need a healthy society. Education, health care, and equal opportunity are essential to a productive workforce. Safe products and working conditions not only attract customers but lower the internal costs of accidents. Efficient utilization of land, water, energy, and other natural resources makes business more productive. Good government, the rule of law, and property rights are essential for efficiency and innovation. Strong regulatory standards protect both consumers and competitive companies from exploitation. Ultimately, a healthy society creates expanding demand for business, as more human needs are met and aspirations grow. Any business that pursues its ends at the expense of the society in which it operates will find its success to be illusory and ultimately temporary.

At the same time, a healthy society needs successful companies. No social program can rival the business sector when it comes to creating the jobs, wealth, and innovation that improve standards of living and social conditions over time. If governments, NGOs, and other participants in civil society weaken the ability of business to operate productively, they may win battles but will lose the war, as corporate and regional competitiveness fade, wages stagnate, jobs disappear, and the wealth that pays taxes and supports nonprofit contributions evaporates.

Leaders in both business and civil society have focused too much on the friction between them and not enough on the points of intersection. The mutual dependence of corporations and society implies that both business decisions and social policies must follow the principle of *shared value*. That is, choices must benefit both sides. If either a business or a society pursues policies that benefit its interests at the expense of the other, it will find itself on a dangerous path. A temporary gain to one will undermine the long-term prosperity of both.[1]

To put these broad principles into practice, a company must integrate a social perspective into the core frameworks it already uses to understand competition and guide its business strategy.

Identifying the Points of Intersection
The interdependence between a company and society takes two forms. First, a company impinges upon society through its operations in the normal course of business: These are *inside-out linkages*.

Virtually every activity in a company's value chain touches on the communities in which the firm operates, creating either positive or negative social consequences. (For an example of this process, see the exhibit "Looking inside out: mapping the social impact of the value chain.") While companies are increasingly aware of the social impact of their activities (such as hiring practices, emissions, and waste disposal), these impacts can be more subtle and variable than many managers realize. For one thing, they depend on location. The same manufacturing operation will have very different social consequences in China than in the United States.

A company's impact on society also changes over time, as social standards evolve and science progresses. Asbestos, now understood as a serious health risk, was thought to be safe in the early 1900s, given the scientific knowledge then available. Evidence of its risks gradually mounted for more than 50 years before any company

Mapping Social Opportunities

The interdependence of a company and society can be analyzed with the same tools used to analyze competitive position and develop strategy. In this way, the firm can focus its particular CSR activities to best effect. Rather than merely acting on well-intentioned impulses or reacting to outside pressure, the organization can set an affirmative CSR agenda that produces maximum social benefit as well as gains for the business.

These two tools should be used in different ways. When a company uses the value chain to chart all the social consequences of its activities, it has, in effect, created an inventory of problems and opportunities—mostly operational issues—that need to be investigated,

was held liable for the harms it can cause. Many firms that failed to anticipate the consequences of this evolving body of research have been bankrupted by the results. No longer can companies be content to monitor only the obvious social impacts of today. Without a careful process for identifying evolving social effects of tomorrow, firms may risk their very survival.

Not only does corporate activity affect society, but external social conditions also influence corporations, for better and for worse. These are *outside-in linkages*.

Every company operates within a competitive context, which significantly affects its ability to carry out its strategy, especially in the long run. Social conditions form a key part of this context. Competitive context garners far less attention than value chain impacts but can have far greater strategic importance for both companies and societies. Ensuring the health of the competitive context benefits both the company and the community.

prioritized, and addressed. In general, companies should attempt to clear away as many negative value-chain social impacts as possible. Some company activities will prove to offer opportunities for social and strategic distinction.

In addressing competitive context, companies cannot take on every area in the diamond. Therefore, the task is to identify those areas of social context with the greatest strategic value. A company should carefully choose from this menu one or a few social initiatives that will have the greatest shared value: benefit for both society and its own competitiveness.

Competitive context can be divided into four broad areas: first, the quantity and quality of available business inputs—human resources, for example, or transportation infrastructure; second, the rules and incentives that govern competition—such as policies that protect intellectual property, ensure transparency, safeguard against corruption, and encourage investment; third, the size and sophistication of local demand, influenced by such things as standards for product quality and safety, consumer rights, and fairness in government purchasing; fourth, the local availability of supporting industries, such as service providers and machinery producers. Any and all of these aspects of context can be opportunities for CSR initiatives. (See the exhibit "Looking outside in: social influences on competitiveness.") The ability to recruit appropriate human resources, for example, may depend on a number of social factors that companies can influence, such as the local educational system, the

Looking inside out: mapping the social impact of the value chain

The value chain depicts all the activities a company engages in while doing business. It can be used as a framework to identify the positive and negative social impact of those activities. These "inside-out" linkages may range from hiring and layoff policies to greenhouse gas emissions, as the partial list of examples illustrated here demonstrates.

- Relationships with universities
- Ethical research practices (e.g., animal testing, GMOs)
- Product safety
- Conservation of raw materials
- Recycling

- Financial reporting practices
- Government practices
- Transparency
- Use of lobbying

- Education & job training
- Safe working conditions
- Diversity & discrimination
- Health care & other benefits
- Compensation policies
- Layoff policies

- Procurement & supply chain practices (e.g., bribery, child labor, conflict diamonds, pricing to farmers)
- Uses of particular inputs (e.g., animal fur)
- Utilization of natural resources

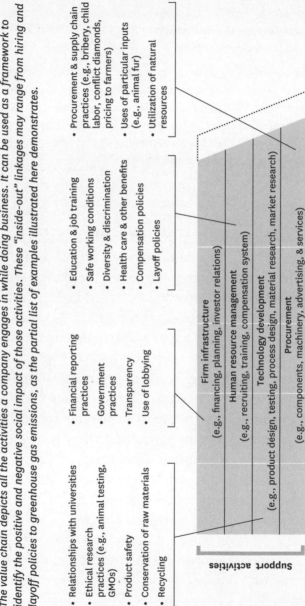

Firm infrastructure
(e.g., financing, planning, investor relations)

Human resource management
(e.g., recruiting, training, compensation system)

Technology development
(e.g., product design, testing, process design, material research, market research)

Procurement
(e.g., components, machinery, advertising, & services)

Support activities

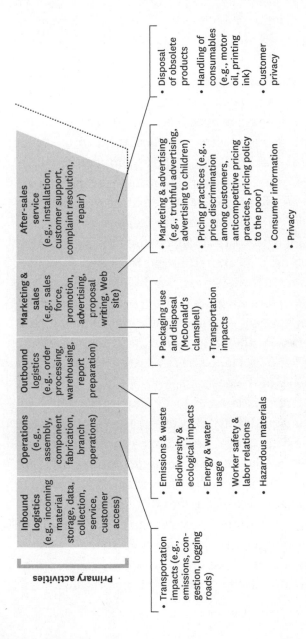

Primary activities

| Inbound logistics (e.g., incoming material storage, data, collection, service, customer access) | Operations (e.g., assembly, component fabrication, branch operations) | Outbound logistics (e.g., order processing, warehousing, report preparation) | Marketing & sales (e.g., sales force, promotion, advertising, proposal writing, Web site) | After-sales service (e.g., installation, customer support, complaint resolution, repair) |

- Transportation impacts (e.g., emissions, congestion, logging roads)

- Emissions & waste
- Biodiversity & ecological impacts
- Energy & water usage
- Worker safety & labor relations
- Hazardous materials

- Packaging use and disposal (McDonald's clamshell)
- Transportation impacts

- Marketing & advertising (e.g., truthful advertising, advertising to children)
- Pricing practices (e.g., price discrimination among customers, anticompetitive pricing practices, pricing policy to the poor)
- Consumer information
- Privacy

- Disposal of obsolete products
- Handling of consumables (e.g., motor oil, printing ink)
- Customer privacy

Source: Michael E. Porter, Competitive Advantage: Creating and Sustaining Superior Performance, 1985

availability of housing, the existence of discrimination (which limits the pool of workers), and the adequacy of the public health infrastructure.[2]

Choosing Which Social Issues to Address

No business can solve all of society's problems or bear the cost of doing so. Instead, each company must select issues that intersect with its particular business. Other social agendas are best left to those companies in other industries, NGOs, or government institutions that are better positioned to address them. The essential test that should guide CSR is not whether a cause is worthy but whether it presents an opportunity to create shared value—that is, a meaningful benefit for society that is also valuable to the business.

Our framework suggests that the social issues affecting a company fall into three categories, which distinguish between the many worthy causes and the narrower set of social issues that are both important and strategic for the business.

Generic social issues may be important to society but are neither significantly affected by the company's operations nor influence the company's long-term competitiveness. *Value chain social impacts* are those that are significantly affected by the company's activities in the ordinary course of business. *Social dimensions of competitive context* are factors in the external environment that significantly affect the underlying drivers of competitiveness in those places where the company operates. (See the exhibit "Prioritizing social issues.")

Looking outside in: social influences on competitiveness

In addition to understanding the social ramifications of the value chain, effective CSR requires an understanding of the social dimensions of the company's competitive context—the "outside-in" linkages that affect its ability to improve productivity and execute strategy. These can be understood using the diamond framework, which shows how the conditions at a company's locations (such as transportation infrastructure and honestly enforced regulatory policy) affect its ability to compete.

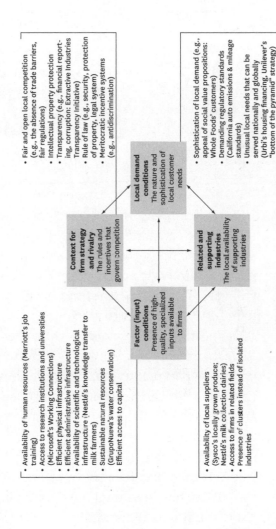

- Availability of human resources (Marriott's job training)
- Access to research institutions and universities (Microsoft's Working Connections)
- Efficient physical infrastructure
- Efficient administrative infrastructure
- Availability of scientific and technological infrastructure (Nestlé's knowledge transfer to milk farmers)
- Sustainable natural resources (GrupoNueva's water conservation)
- Efficient access to capital

Factor (input) conditions
Presence of high-quality, specialized inputs available to firms

Context for firm strategy and rivalry
The rules and incentives that govern competition

- Fair and open local competition (e.g., the absence of trade barriers, fair regulations)
- Intellectual property protection
- Transparency (e.g., financial reporting, corruption: Extractive Industries Transparency Initiative)
- Rule of law (e.g., security, protection of property, legal system)
- Meritocratic incentive systems (e.g., antidiscrimination)

Local demand conditions
The nature and sophistication of local customer needs

- Sophistication of local demand (e.g., appeal of social value propositions: Whole Foods' customers)
- Demanding regulatory standards (California auto emissions & mileage standards)
- Unusual local needs that can be served nationally and globally (Urbi's housing financing, Unilever's "bottom of the pyramid" strategy)

Related and supporting industries
The local availability of supporting industries

- Availability of local suppliers (Sysco's locally grown produce; Nestlé's milk collection dairies)
- Access to firms in related fields
- Presence of clusters instead of isolated industries

Source: Michael E. Porter, The Competitive Advantage of Nations, 1990

Prioritizing social issues

Generic social issues	Value chain social impacts	Social dimensions of competitive context
Social issues that are not significantly affected by a company's operations nor materially affect its long-term competitiveness.	Social issues that are significantly affected by a company's activities in the ordinary course of business.	Social issues in the external environment that significantly affect the underlying drivers of a company's competitiveness in the locations where it operates.

Every company will need to sort social issues into these three categories for each of its business units and primary locations, then rank them in terms of potential impact. Into which category a given social issue falls will vary from business unit to business unit, industry to industry, and place to place.

Supporting a dance company may be a generic social issue for a utility like Southern California Edison but an important part of the competitive context for a corporation like American Express, which depends on the high-end entertainment, hospitality, and tourism cluster. Carbon emissions may be a generic social issue for a financial services firm like Bank of America, a negative value chain impact for a transportation-based company like UPS, or both a value chain impact and a competitive context issue for a car manufacturer like Toyota. The AIDS pandemic in Africa may be a generic social issue for a U.S. retailer like Home Depot, a value chain impact for a pharmaceutical company like GlaxoSmithKline, and a competitive context issue for a mining company like Anglo American that depends on local labor in Africa for its operations.

Even issues that apply widely in the economy, such as diversity in hiring or conservation of energy, can have greater significance for some industries than for others. Health care benefits, for example, will present fewer challenges for software development or biotechnology firms, where workforces tend to be small and well compensated, than for companies in a field like retailing, which is heavily dependent on large numbers of lower-wage workers.

Within an industry, a given social issue may cut differently for different companies, owing to differences in competitive positioning. In the auto industry, for example, Volvo has chosen to make safety a central element of its competitive positioning, while Toyota has built a competitive advantage from the environmental benefits of its hybrid technology. For an individual company, some issues will prove to be important for many of its business units and locations, offering opportunities for strategic corporatewide CSR initiatives.

Where a social issue is salient for many companies across multiple industries, it can often be addressed most effectively through cooperative models. The Extractive Industries Transparency Initiative, for example, includes 19 major oil, gas, and mining companies that have agreed to discourage corruption through full public disclosure and verification of all corporate payments to governments in the countries in which they operate. Collective action by all major corporations in these industries prevents corrupt governments from undermining social benefit by simply choosing not to deal with the firms that disclose their payments.

Creating a Corporate Social Agenda

Categorizing and ranking social issues is just the means to an end, which is to create an explicit and affirmative corporate social agenda. A corporate social agenda looks beyond community expectations to opportunities to achieve social and economic benefits simultaneously. It moves from mitigating harm to finding ways to reinforce corporate strategy by advancing social conditions.

Such a social agenda must be responsive to stakeholders, but it cannot stop there. A substantial portion of corporate resources and attention must migrate to truly strategic CSR. (See the exhibit "Corporate involvement in society: a strategic approach.") It is through strategic CSR that the company will make the most significant social impact and reap the greatest business benefits.

Responsive CSR. Responsive CSR comprises two elements: acting as a good corporate citizen, attuned to the evolving social concerns of stakeholders, and mitigating existing or anticipated adverse effects from business activities.

Good citizenship is a sine qua non of CSR, and companies need to do it well. Many worthy local organizations rely on corporate contributions, while employees derive justifiable pride from their company's positive involvement in the community.

Corporate involvement in society: a strategic approach

Generic social impacts	Value chain social impacts	Social dimensions of competitive context
Good citizenship	Mitigate harm from value chain activities	Strategic philanthropy that leverages capabilities to improve salient areas of competitive context
Responsive CSR	Transform value-chain activities to benefit society while reinforcing strategy	Strategic CSR

The best corporate citizenship initiatives involve far more than writing a check: They specify clear, measurable goals and track results over time. A good example is GE's program to adopt underperforming public high schools near several of its major U.S. facilities. The company contributes between $250,000 and $1 million over a five-year period to each school and makes in-kind donations as well. GE managers and employees take an active role by working with school administrators to assess needs and mentor or tutor students. In an independent study of ten schools in the program between 1989 and 1999, nearly all showed significant improvement, while the graduation rate in four of the five worst-performing schools doubled from an average of 30% to 60%.

Effective corporate citizenship initiatives such as this one create goodwill and improve relations with local governments and other important constituencies. What's more, GE's employees feel great pride in their participation. Their effect is inherently limited, however. No matter how beneficial the program is, it remains incidental to the company's business, and the direct effect on GE's recruiting and retention is modest.

The second part of responsive CSR—mitigating the harm arising from a firm's value chain activities—is essentially an operational challenge. Because there are a myriad of possible value chain impacts for each business unit, many companies have adopted a checklist approach to CSR, using standardized sets of social and environmental risks. The Global Reporting Initiative, which is rapidly becoming a standard for CSR reporting, has enumerated a list of 141 CSR issues, supplemented by auxiliary lists for different industries.

These lists make for an excellent starting point, but companies need a more proactive and tailored internal process. Managers at each business unit can use the value chain as a tool to identify systematically the social impacts of the unit's activities in each location. Here operating management, which is closest to the work actually being done, is particularly helpful. Most challenging is to anticipate impacts that are not yet well recognized. Consider B&Q, an international chain of home supply centers based in England. The company has begun to analyze systematically tens of thousands of products in its hundreds of stores against a list of a dozen social issues—from climate change to working conditions at its suppliers' factories—to determine which products pose potential social responsibility risks and how the company might take action before any external pressure is brought to bear.

For most value chain impacts, there is no need to reinvent the wheel. The company should identify best practices for dealing with each one, with an eye toward how those practices are changing. Some companies will be more proactive and effective in mitigating the wide array of social problems that the value chain can create. These companies will gain an edge, but—just as for procurement and other operational improvements—any advantage is likely to be temporary.

Strategic CSR. For any company, strategy must go beyond best practices. It is about choosing a unique position—doing things differently from competitors in a way that lowers costs or better serves a particular set of customer needs. These principles apply to a company's relationship to society as readily as to its relationship to its customers and rivals.

Strategic CSR moves beyond good corporate citizenship and mitigating harmful value chain impacts to mount a small number of initiatives whose social and business benefits are large and distinctive. Strategic CSR involves both inside-out and outside-in dimensions working in tandem. It is here that the opportunities for shared value truly lie.

Many opportunities to pioneer innovations to benefit both society and a company's own competitiveness can arise in the product offering and the value chain. Toyota's response to concerns over automobile emissions is an example. Toyota's Prius, the hybrid electric/gasoline vehicle, is the first in a series of innovative car models that have produced competitive advantage and environmental benefits. Hybrid engines emit as little as 10% of the harmful pollutants conventional vehicles produce while consuming only half as much gas. Voted 2004 Car of the Year by *Motor Trend* magazine, Prius has given Toyota a lead so substantial that Ford and other car companies are licensing the technology. Toyota has created a unique position with customers and is well on its way to establishing its technology as the world standard.

Urbi, a Mexican construction company, has prospered by building housing for disadvantaged buyers using novel financing vehicles such as flexible mortgage payments made through payroll deductions. Crédit Agricole, France's largest bank, has differentiated itself by offering specialized financial products related to the environment, such as financing packages for energy-saving home improvements and for audits to certify farms as organic.

Strategic CSR also unlocks shared value by investing in social aspects of context that strengthen company competitiveness. A symbiotic relationship develops: The success of the company and the success of the community become mutually reinforcing. Typically, the more closely tied a social issue is to the company's business, the greater the opportunity to leverage the firm's resources and capabilities, and benefit society.

Microsoft's Working Connections partnership with the American Association of Community Colleges

(AACC) is a good example of a shared-value opportunity arising from investments in context. The shortage of information technology workers is a significant constraint on Microsoft's growth; currently, there are more than 450,000 unfilled IT positions in the United States alone. Community colleges, with an enrollment of 11.6 million students, representing 45% of all U.S. undergraduates, could be a major solution. Microsoft recognizes, however, that community colleges face special challenges: IT curricula are not standardized, technology used in classrooms is often outdated, and there are no systematic professional development programs to keep faculty up to date.

Microsoft's $50 million five-year initiative was aimed at all three problems. In addition to contributing money and products, Microsoft sent employee volunteers to colleges to assess needs, contribute to curriculum development, and create faculty development institutes. Note that in this case, volunteers and assigned staff were able to use their core professional skills to address a social need, a far cry from typical volunteer programs. Microsoft has achieved results that have benefited many communities while having a direct—and potentially significant—impact on the company.

Integrating Inside-Out and Outside-In Practices

Pioneering value chain innovations and addressing social constraints to competitiveness are each powerful tools for creating economic and social value. However, as our examples illustrate, the impact is even greater if they work together. Activities in the value chain can be performed in ways that reinforce improvements in the social dimensions of context. At the same time, investments in competitive context have the potential to reduce constraints on a company's value chain activities. Marriott, for example, provides 180 hours of paid classroom and on-the-job training to chronically unemployed job candidates. The company has combined this with support for local community service organizations, which identify, screen, and refer the candidates to Marriott. The net result is both a major benefit to communities and a reduction in Marriott's cost of recruiting entry-level employees. Ninety percent of those in the training program take jobs with Marriott. One year later, more than 65% are still in their jobs, a substantially higher retention rate than the norm.

When value chain practices and investments in competitive context are fully integrated, CSR becomes hard to distinguish from the day-to-day business of the company. Nestlé, for example, works directly with small farmers in developing countries to source the basic commodities, such as milk, coffee, and cocoa, on which much of its global business depends. (See the sidebar "Integrating Company Practice and Context: Nestlé's Milk District.") The company's investment in local infrastructure and its transfer of world-class knowledge and technology over decades has produced enormous social benefits through improved health care, better education, and economic development, while giving Nestlé direct and reliable access to the commodities it needs to maintain a profitable global business. Nestlé's distinctive strategy is inseparable from its social impact.

Creating a Social Dimension to the Value Proposition

At the heart of any strategy is a unique value proposition: a set of needs a company can meet for its chosen customers that others cannot. The most strategic CSR occurs when a company adds a social dimension to its value proposition, making social impact integral to the overall strategy.

Consider Whole Foods Market, whose value proposition is to sell organic, natural, and healthy food products to customers who are passionate about food and the environment. Social issues are fundamental to what makes Whole Foods unique in food retailing and to its ability to command premium prices. The company's sourcing emphasizes purchases from local farmers through each store's procurement process. Buyers screen out foods containing any of nearly 100 common ingredients that the company considers unhealthy or environmentally damaging. The same standards apply to products made internally. Whole Foods' baked goods, for example, use only unbleached and unbromated flour.

Whole Foods' commitment to natural and environmentally friendly operating practices extends well beyond sourcing. Stores are constructed using a minimum of virgin raw materials. Recently, the company purchased renewable wind energy credits equal to 100% of its electricity use in all of its stores and facilities, the only *Fortune* 500 company to offset its electricity consumption entirely. Spoiled produce and biodegradable waste are trucked to regional centers for composting. Whole Foods' vehicles are being converted to run on

Integrating Company Practice and Context: Nestlé's Milk District

Nestlé's approach to working with small farmers exemplifies the symbiotic relationship between social progress and competitive advantage. Ironically, while the company's reputation remains marred by a 30-year-old controversy surrounding sales of infant formula in Africa, the corporation's impact in developing countries has often been profoundly positive.

Consider the history of Nestlé's milk business in India. In 1962, the company wanted to enter the Indian market, and it received government permission to build a dairy in the northern district of Moga. Poverty in the region was severe; people were without electricity, transportation, telephones, or medical care. A farmer typically owned less than five acres of poorly irrigated and infertile soil. Many kept a single buffalo cow that produced just enough milk for their own consumption. Sixty percent of calves died newborn. Because farmers lacked refrigeration, transportation, or any way to test for quality, milk could not travel far and was frequently contaminated or diluted.

Nestlé came to Moga to build a business, not to engage in CSR. But Nestlé's value chain, derived from the company's origins in Switzerland, depended on establishing local sources of milk from a large, diversified base of small farmers. Establishing that value chain in Moga required Nestlé to transform the competitive context in ways that created tremendous shared value for both the company and the region.

Nestlé built refrigerated dairies as collection points for milk in each town and sent its trucks out to the dairies to collect the milk. With the trucks went veterinarians, nutritionists, agronomists, and quality assurance experts. Medicines and nutritional supplements were provided for sick animals, and monthly training sessions were held for local farmers. Farmers learned that the milk quality depended on the cows' diet, which in turn depended on adequate feed crop irrigation. With financing and technical assistance from Nestlé, farmers began to dig previously unaffordable deep-bore wells. Improved irrigation not only fed cows but increased crop yields, producing surplus wheat and rice and raising the standard of living.

When Nestlé's milk factory first opened, only 180 local farmers supplied milk. Today, Nestlé buys milk from more than 75,000 farmers in the region, collecting it twice daily from more than 650 village dairies. The death rate of calves has dropped by 75%. Milk production has increased 50-fold. As the quality has improved, Nestlé has been able to pay higher prices to farmers than those set by the government, and its steady biweekly payments have enabled farmers to obtain credit. Competing dairies and milk factories have opened, and an industry cluster is beginning to develop.

Today, Moga has a significantly higher standard of living than other regions in the vicinity. Ninety percent of the homes have electricity, and most have telephones; all villages have primary schools, and many have secondary schools. Moga has five times the number of doctors as neighboring regions. The increased purchasing power of local farmers has also greatly expanded the market for Nestlé's products, further supporting the firm's economic success.

Nestlé's commitment to working with small farmers is central to its strategy. It enables the company to obtain a stable supply of high-quality commodities without paying middlemen. The corporation's other core products—coffee and cocoa—are often grown by small farmers in developing countries under similar conditions. Nestlé's experience in setting up collection points, training farmers, and introducing better technology in Moga has been repeated in Brazil, Thailand, and a dozen other countries, including, most recently, China. In each case, as Nestlé has prospered, so has the community.

biofuels. Even the cleaning products used in its stores are environmentally friendly. And through its philanthropy, the company has created the Animal Compassion Foundation to develop more natural and humane ways of raising farm animals. In short, nearly every aspect of the company's value chain reinforces the social dimensions of its value proposition, distinguishing Whole Foods from its competitors.

Not every company can build its entire value proposition around social issues as Whole Foods does, but adding a social dimension to the value proposition offers a new frontier in competitive positioning. Government regulation, exposure to criticism and liability, and consumers' attention to social issues are all persistently increasing. As a result, the number of industries and companies whose competitive advantage can involve social value propositions is constantly growing. Sysco, for example, the largest distributor of food products to restaurants and institutions in North America, has begun an initiative to preserve small, family-owned farms and offer locally grown produce to its customers as a source of competitive differentiation. Even large global multinationals—such as General Electric, with its "ecomagination" initiative that focuses on developing water purification technology and other "green" businesses, and Unilever, through its efforts to pioneer new products, packaging, and distribution systems to meet the needs of the poorest populations—have decided that major business opportunities lie in integrating business and society.

Organizing for CSR

Integrating business and social needs takes more than good intentions and strong leadership. It requires adjustments in organization, reporting relationships, and incentives. Few companies have engaged operating management in processes that identify and prioritize social issues based on their salience to business operations and their importance to the company's competitive context. Even fewer have unified their philanthropy with the management of their CSR efforts, much less sought to embed a social dimension into their core value proposition. Doing these things requires a far different approach to both CSR and philanthropy than the one prevalent today. Companies must shift from a fragmented, defensive posture to an integrated, affirmative approach. The focus must move away from an emphasis on image to an emphasis on substance.

The current preoccupation with measuring stakeholder satisfaction has it backwards. What needs to be measured is social impact. Operating managers must understand the importance of the outside-in influence of competitive context, while people with responsibility for CSR initiatives must have a granular understanding of every activity in the value chain. Value chain and competitive-context investments in CSR need to be incorporated into the performance measures of managers with P&L responsibility. These transformations require more than a broadening of job definition; they require overcoming a number of long-standing prejudices. Many operating managers have developed an ingrained us-versus-them mind-set that responds defensively to the discussion of any social issue, just as many NGOs view askance the pursuit of social value for profit. These attitudes must change if companies want to leverage the social dimension of corporate strategy.

Strategy is always about making choices, and success in corporate social responsibility is no different. It is about choosing which social issues to focus on. The short-term performance pressures companies face rule out indiscriminate investments in social value creation. They suggest, instead, that creating shared value should be viewed like research and development, as a long-term investment in a company's future competitiveness. The billions of dollars already being spent on CSR and corporate philanthropy would generate far more benefit to both business and society if consistently invested using the principles we have outlined.

While responsive CSR depends on being a good corporate citizen and addressing every social harm the business creates, strategic CSR is far more selective. Companies are called on to address hundreds of social issues, but only a few represent opportunities to make a real difference to society or to confer a competitive advantage. Organizations that make the right choices and build focused, proactive, and integrated social initiatives in concert with their core strategies will increasingly distance themselves from the pack.

The Moral Purpose of Business

By providing jobs, investing capital, purchasing goods, and doing business every day, corporations have a profound and positive influence on society. The most important thing a corporation can do for society, and for any community, is contribute to a prosperous economy. Governments and NGOs often forget this basic truth. When developing countries distort rules and incentives for business, for example, they penalize productive companies. Such countries are doomed to poverty, low wages, and selling off their natural resources. Corporations have the know-how and resources to change this state of affairs, not only in the developing world but also in economically disadvantaged communities in advanced economies.

This cannot excuse businesses that seek short-term profits deceptively or shirk the social and environmental consequences of their actions. But CSR should not be only about what businesses have done that is wrong—important as that is. Nor should it be only about making philanthropic contributions to local charities, lending a hand in time of disaster, or providing relief to society's needy—worthy though these contributions may be. Efforts to find shared value in operating practices and in the social dimensions of competitive context have the potential not only to foster economic and social development but to change the way companies and society think about each other. NGOs, governments, and companies must stop thinking in terms of "corporate social responsibility" and start thinking in terms of "corporate social integration."

Perceiving social responsibility as building shared value rather than as damage control or as a PR campaign will require dramatically different thinking in business. We are convinced, however, that CSR will become increasingly important to competitive success.

Corporations are not responsible for all the world's problems, nor do they have the resources to solve them all. Each company can identify the particular set of societal problems that it is best equipped to help resolve and from which it can gain the greatest competitive benefit. Addressing social issues by creating shared value will lead to self-sustaining solutions that do not depend on private or government subsidies. When a well-run business applies its vast resources, expertise, and management talent to problems that it understands and in which it has a stake, it can have a greater impact on social good than any other institution or philanthropic organization.

Notes

1. An early discussion of the idea of CSR as an opportunity rather than a cost can be found in David Grayson and Adrian Hodges, *Corporate Social Opportunity* (Greenleaf, 2004).

2. For a more complete discussion of the importance of competitive context and the diamond model, see Michael E. Porter and Mark R. Kramer, "The Competitive Advantage of Corporate Philanthropy," HBR December 2002. See also Michael Porter's book *The Competitive Advantage of Nations* (The Free Press, 1990) and his article "Locations, Clusters, and Company Strategy," in *The Oxford Handbook of Economic Geography,* edited by Gordon L. Clark, Maryann P. Feldman, and Meric S. Gertler (Oxford University Press, 2000).

MICHAEL E. PORTER is the Bishop William Lawrence University Professor at Harvard Business School. **MARK R. KRAMER** is the managing director of FSG Social Impact Advisors, an international nonprofit consulting firm.

Originally published in December 2006. Reprint R0612D

The Greening of Petrobras

by José Sergio Gabrielli de Azevedo

HOW CAN PETROBRAS, A huge multinational whose main expertise is offshore drilling, evangelize about protecting the environment? I know it might seem preposterous—particularly since Petrobras was making headlines not too long ago for a string of environmental disasters.

In January 2000, a leak in a corroded pipeline spilled 350,000 gallons of crude oil into Guanabara Bay, a tourist destination, fishing community, and wildlife habitat near Rio de Janeiro, which had already suffered a Petrobras spill in 1997. Because the pipe didn't have modern sensors, oil poured out for two hours before the leak was detected. We were fined more than $25 million. Environmental groups were furious. Local fishermen protested outside our headquarters here in Rio and Greenpeace activists chained themselves to railings outside the building and left oil-soaked dead birds at its entrance. Then, just six months later we had an even bigger leak at a refinery near Curitiba—a million gallons of oil poured into two rivers. We were criticized again for outdated leak-detection technology, as well as for inadequate staffing and emergency plans, and were fined $115 million. Those accidents, along with others that year, generated a flood of bad press, including the BBC's derisive comment that Petrobras showed "an embarrassing level of incompetence." The incidents were environmentally devastating, alarming to our investors, harmful to our bottom line, bad for the company's image, and demoralizing for employees and all Brazilians.

We thought we'd seen the worst of it, but that disastrous period was capped by the sinking of our P-36 oil platform in March 2001. The $350 million rig was the world's largest floating production platform, and it stood as a symbol of our—and Brazil's—ambitions and technical prowess. Two explosions on the platform killed 11 of our employees, and after several days it sank, leaking more than 300,000 gallons of oil.

That was then.

We haven't had a major accident in eight years, and today we're acknowledged as a global leader in sustainability practices. We're a member of the World Business Council for Sustainable Development and the United Nations Global Compact, a social and environmental policy program, where I sit on the board. We're listed on the Dow Jones Sustainability Index, our social and environmental report recently received the Global Reporting Initiative's highest rating for transparency, and this year the research and rating firm Management

Idea in Brief

Over the past eight years Brazilian energy giant Petrobras has transformed itself from a notorious environmental offender into a global leader in sustainability. In this article the CEO, a onetime leftist activist who believes business should drive social improvement, describes how the company turned itself around. When Gabrielli took the reins, Petrobras was coming out of a tumultuous period. The state-owned monopoly had become a publicly traded corporation competing in an open market, and its operations were expanding rapidly. During this time a series of disastrous oil spills and accidents took place. In response, Philippe Reichstul, one of Gabrielli's predecessors, launched a $4 billion program for environmental and operational safety, comprising more than 4,000 projects. Under Gabrielli's stewardship, the company approached environmental performance issues in three ways: improving its own culture and operations, influ-

encing its suppliers, and championing renewable-energy development. At the center of its strategy is a program built on a set of requirements for performance in 15 areas. Among them is the stipulation that Petrobras's managers lead by example. Environmental policy is a boardroom consideration, and the company's top managers visibly demonstrate their commitment by joining the teams that go out into the field to audit health, environmental, and safety compliance. Promoting environmentally sound behavior outside the company is another key requirement. To this end, Petrobras is pitting the firm's thousands of Brazilian suppliers against one another in a battle to see who's greenest. The company has devised a system to measure and monitor their environmental performance—and awards contracts to the high scorers. It has also set its sights on becoming a world leader in biofuel, building a huge R&D network that stretches across Brazil and around the globe.

& Excellence ranked us number one among the world's oil and gas companies for sustainability.

There's a metaphor in business about turning the tanker around. We did it with an entire oil company.

Setting the Goal

Since its founding as a state-owned firm in 1953, Petrobras has been deeply connected to Brazil's development, and our company culture has been intertwined with our national values. Generally speaking, the culture of Brazil is less individualistic and more social in its outlook than the cultures of many Western countries. Brazilians' sense of being part of a greater whole infuses the company and has been strengthened by our efforts to overcome enormous challenges. I didn't create this spirit, but as CEO, I'm its steward.

When I took the reins as CEO in 2005, we were coming out of a tumultuous transitional period. In the late 1990s the company began its transformation from a state firm with a national monopoly on oil exploration and production to a quasi-governmental entity with 60% of its equity capital traded on the Bovespa and the New York Stock Exchange and a market fully open to outside competitors. Petrobras was facing new competitive pressures, new stakeholders, and a new emphasis on profits and growth. During the past 10 years, we've doubled oil production, increased reserves by more than 75%, and expanded operations into 27 countries. It was when we were revving up growth that the spills and platform disaster rocked the company.

In response to the Guanabara Bay and Curitiba spills, Philippe Reichstul, who was CEO from 1999 until 2001, created a new director-level position for health, safety, and environment and launched the Program for Excellence in Environmental and Operational Safety

Management. PEGASO, as we called it, was a $4 billion initiative encompassing more than 4,000 separate projects designed to prevent accidents. It was the biggest environmental and operational safety program ever launched in Brazil. But PEGASO wasn't just a risk management program. It was central to a new strategy to turn our reputation around and become an industry benchmark for environmental performance. That was a pretty audacious goal, given our recent history.

I joined Petrobras as director of finance and investor relations in 2003, when the company's social and environmental initiatives were aggressively expanding under the direction of my predecessor, José Eduardo Dutra. I was keenly attuned to their importance. From a purely financial perspective, environmental mismanagement was just bad business. From an investor relations perspective, ignoring the growing demand for transparency and sustainability was also clearly bad business. And, from a personal perspective, the company's new sustainability strategies mirrored my own beliefs, rooted in my political and academic past.

In the late 1960s, I'd been a prominent activist in the student movement that was challenging Brazil's dictatorship—prominent enough that the army threw me in jail in 1970. After I was released, I gravitated toward a group of intellectuals, academics, and union leaders, including Luiz Inácio Lula da Silva (now Brazil's president), and in 1980 I helped found the Workers' Party. My progressive, leftist political orientation certainly colors how I think about Petrobras's role in Brazil and the world and, more broadly, how I view the legitimacy of business—its social license to operate. My academic work also has reflected this social orientation. I'm actually a professor on leave from the Federal University of Bahia. I received my PhD in economics from Boston University in 1987 and went on to become the director of the faculty of economics at my university. My research, writing, and teaching, which have always focused on macroeconomics, labor markets, and regional development, crystallized my views about the responsibility and the power of business to drive social improvement. Private enterprise, of course, is responsible to shareholders, but supporting sustainability goals is not at odds with that. It's complementary—and necessary.

Improving Performance Inside

As CEO, I approach environmental performance issues in three broad ways: improving our own culture and operations, influencing—indeed, pressuring—the companies that do business with us, and championing renewable-energy development.

At the center of our internal strategy is our health, safety, and environment program. It's a huge operation—we invested $2.5 billion in HSE this year. The program is built on a set of guidelines for required performance in 15 areas, such as leadership, regulatory compliance, risk evaluation and management, training, and accident analysis—guidelines that would be familiar to most big companies. Among them are the requirements that Petrobras's managers lead by example, assess the environmental impact of new projects, monitor and reduce the impact of ongoing company activities, and implement programs promoting environmental behavior inside and outside the company. One of our goals, which we've almost met, is to certify the compliance of all our units with international health, safety, and environmental standards, including the best-practice standard for environmental management, ISO 14001. Having this certification sends a message about our seriousness and competence, which is crucial as we try to influence our partners.

HSE compliance may sound dry and technical and perhaps only of concern to middle managers. And, yes, managers are the ones who execute much of this. But the HSE policy is an explicit component of our strategic plan. I bring consideration of this policy right into the boardroom, and, with my six colleagues on the executive board, review and approve the guidelines.

My top managers and I are visibly committed to this policy. For instance, we have joined the auditing teams that check the HSE compliance of our business and service units and new projects. Senior, executive, and general managers have participated in more than 1,000 audits, going on field trips to refineries, offshore platforms, and pipelines. I myself or one of the Petrobras directors joined 28 of these site visits. When I step off the helicopter at an offshore platform, it's sort of like the general showing up at the barracks for the morning bed check. But employees know that I'm there because I care about what they're doing, not to catch some indiscretion. This is part of an important formal and informal trickling-down process that drives the cultural change into day-to-day operations.

As every chief executive knows, striking the right balance between formality and informality can be tricky. By nature I'm an informal person. I prefer simple, inexpensive restaurants where the locals go. I dress in jeans on casual Fridays and often wear my photo ID tag, like any other employee. I think that style helps me communicate with employees at all levels. It's authentic, and they know it. But being informal on occasion doesn't mean I'm soft on people. I have high expectations, and I'm clear about them. In meetings with my senior staff members, I ask a lot of questions, and they know they'd better be well prepared on their subject, because I will be. If someone's presenting a problem, I want to hear his or her solutions— and succinctly. I keep my PowerPoint presentations to 20 minutes and expect others to be just as efficient. I believe people would say I'm a collegial leader—I work with my senior executives rather than direct them. But when I think a command-and-control approach is expedient, I'll take it. For example, we recently needed to send a representative from Petrobras management to a potentially hostile oil-industry union meeting. We could have sent our HR director or another manager, but I thought the union needed to hear directly from me. So off I went.

Raising the Bar Outside

Companies compete aggressively for our contracts because we're one of the biggest firms in the region. We give preference to the domestic market because, though we're quasi-public, we still have a nationalistic zeal about Brazilian development. In 2007, 70% of the $40 billion we spent on goods and services went to approximately 4,000 domestic suppliers.

Now, any company is going to ask that its suppliers and contractors meet legal, financial, and technical requirements. Yet, like companies anywhere, Brazilian suppliers often won't go beyond minimum legal requirements unless they have clear incentives to do so. Given our size and clout, we realized that we could promote improved social and environmental performance in companies throughout Brazil by giving the highest performers our business.

To that end, shortly after we joined the Global Compact in 2003, we launched Progefe, a program that encourages suppliers and other partners to adopt the Compact's 10 principles. The program also obliges suppliers to strive to come up to our level of HSE and social responsibility performance.

To motivate them, we devised a scoring system to measure and monitor their adherence to health, safety, and environmental standards and rank them according to the maturity of their HSE systems. Suppliers must register with our supplier database and complete a standardized self-assessment of environmental and social performance. Then they have to undergo our own assessment, which for critical service providers includes an on-site evaluation. We often deny low scorers contracts, but they can make changes to improve their scores and bid again. Because of the fierce rivalry for our business, our suppliers tend to engage in continual HSE improvement in order to outscore their competitors. And because of this pressure, the number of our suppliers with ISO environmental certification has grown from 30 to 600 in the past four years. That's good progress, but I'd like to see all our suppliers reach that level.

Leading the Shift

Improving operations—our own and others'—goes only so far in reducing environmental impact. I'm well aware that even if we don't have accidents and we minimize the impact of building and operating pipelines, platforms, and wells, our products put a lot of carbon into the atmosphere when people use them. Now, we're not going to stop producing oil. Our long-term plan is to become one of the five largest integrated energy companies in the world. With the recent Tupi oil field discovery, which adds 5 billion to 8 billion barrels to our reserves, we expect to nearly double our production, to 3.5 million barrels a day by 2012, which will put us in the same league as Exxon.

Yet oil is a finite resource. Renewable energy is not going to replace fossil fuels anytime soon, but it will make up a growing part of the world's energy supply and will be critical in efforts to reduce carbon emissions. As the mix of fuels the world uses changes, I expect Petrobras to drive that shift rather than react to it.

Becoming a world leader in biofuels is an explicit part of our strategy. Between now and 2012, we've earmarked $1.5 billion for biofuel development. It's a principal focus of our CENPES research and development

center, which, though it is already the largest technology R&D facility in South America, is undergoing a
major expansion. The projects we're leading include the
development of second-generation biofuels, such as
ethanol from agribusiness waste, in Brazil. In 2007 we
launched the first pilot plant for producing ethanol
from lignocellulose using enzyme technology. We're
also working on a variety of ways to make existing fuels
burn cleaner.

As an academic, I have a personal fondness for the
center because it strikes a great balance between basic
and applied research, something I've always tried to do
as an economist. CENPES is like the School of Sagres,
which legend has it was founded by the fifteenth-cen-
tury Portuguese explorer Prince Henry to teach the art
of sailing and navigation. Sagres combined the operational expertise of sailors with the knowledge of academics and the dreams of cartographers, just as
CENPES brings together practical and academic knowledge and innovative, exploratory thinking. Unlike
Sagres, though, CENPES sits at the hub of a research
network that stretches across Brazil and around the
globe. I'm sure Prince Henry would have created such a
network if he could have. We have contracts to do joint
projects, research, and technology exchanges with 170
Brazilian universities and research centers and more
than 70 international institutions. This is another way
that Petrobras is an engine of change throughout Brazil,
by pushing partners to develop their R&D capabilities in
the same way we push them to improve their environmental and social performance.

Investing Wisely

I've focused on the story of our environmental initiatives here because the arc of the narrative is so clear, from the catastrophes at the start of the decade to our recovery and, now, leadership. But in actuality, we don't compartmentalize environmental stewardship—and I think any company would be unwise to do so. It's integrated into our broader CSR and sustainability strategy, which includes good corporate governance, transparency, and investments in social development, particularly in Brazil.

The economic downturn will force us to reevaluate our allocation of capital, certainly for the near term. We may have to temporarily reduce some investment spending across our business lines, until capital markets and oil prices recover. But as we prioritize our capital investments, I will protect the budgets required to meet our environmental goals and will continue to champion our commitment to sustainable development, leading by example. Our shareholders, and society, should expect nothing less.

JOSÉ SERGIO GABRIELLI DE AZEVEDO is the president and CEO of Petrobras, headquartered in Rio de Janeiro.

Originally published in March 2009. Reprint R0903B

A Road Map for Natural Capitalism

by Amory B. Lovins, L. Hunter Lovins, and Paul Hawken

ON SEPTEMBER 16, 1991, a small group of scientists was sealed inside Biosphere II, a glittering 3.2-acre glass and metal dome in Oracle, Arizona. Two years later, when the radical attempt to replicate the earth's main ecosystems in miniature ended, the engineered environment was dying. The gaunt researchers had survived only because fresh air had been pumped in. Despite $200 million worth of elaborate equipment, Biosphere II had failed to generate breathable air, drinkable water, and adequate food for just eight people. Yet Biosphere I, the planet we all inhabit, effortlessly performs those tasks every day for 6 billion of us.

Disturbingly, Biosphere I is now itself at risk. The earth's ability to sustain life, and therefore economic activity, is threatened by the way we extract, process, transport, and dispose of a vast flow of resources—some 220 billion tons a year, or more than 20 times the average American's body weight every day. With dangerously narrow focus, our industries look only at the exploitable resources of the earth's ecosystems—its oceans, forests, and plains—and not at the larger services that those systems provide for free. Resources and ecosystem services both come from the earth—even from the same biological systems—but they're two different things. Forests, for instance, not only produce the resource of wood fiber but also provide such ecosystem services as water storage, habitat, and regulation of the atmosphere and climate. Yet companies that earn income from harvesting the wood fiber resource often do so in ways that damage the forest's ability to carry out its other vital tasks.

Unfortunately, the cost of destroying ecosystem services becomes apparent only when the services start to break down. In China's Yangtze basin in 1998, for example, deforestation triggered flooding that killed 3,700 people, dislocated 223 million, and inundated 60 million acres of cropland. That $30 billion disaster forced a logging moratorium and a $12 billion crash program of reforestation.

The reason companies (and governments) are so prodigal with ecosystem services is that the value of those services doesn't appear on the business balance sheet. But that's a staggering omission. The economy, after all, is embedded in the environment. Recent calculations published in the journal *Nature* conservatively estimate the value of all the earth's ecosystem services to be at least $33 trillion a year. That's close to the gross world product, and it implies a capitalized book value on the order of half a quadrillion dollars.

Idea in Brief

The earth's ability to sustain life is in peril—as companies consume natural resources in ways that prevent ecosystems from regenerating our air, water, and food supplies. For example, clear-cutting forests for wood fiber damages forests' ability to store water, provide animal habitats, and regulate climate.

Why such rampant exploitation? Unlike the value derived from consuming natural resources, the value of ecosystems' most crucial services don't appear on balance sheets. Yet that value is worth $33 trillion a year.

You can capture some of that $33 trillion *and* help restore the planet by practicing **natural capitalism**—conducting business profitably while also protecting natural resources. Some strategies suggested by Amory Lovins, Hunter Lovins, and Paul Hawken: Adopt technologies that extend natural resources' usefulness. Design production systems that eliminate costly waste. And reinvest in nature's capital; for instance, by planting trees to offset power-plant carbon emissions.

Work *with* nature, and you boost profitability—pulling ahead of rivals who continue to work *against* nature.

What's more, for most of these services, there is no known substitute at any price, and we can't live without them.

This article puts forward a new approach not only for protecting the biosphere but also for improving profits and competitiveness. Some very simple changes to the way we run our businesses, built on advanced techniques for making resources more productive, can yield startling benefits both for today's shareholders and for future generations.

This approach is called *natural capitalism* because it's what capitalism might become if its largest category

Idea in Practice

The authors recommend these steps to natural capitalism.

Increase Natural Resources' Productivity

Develop dramatically more efficient production processes that stretch natural resources—energy, minerals, water, forests—5, 10, even 100 times further than they go today. You'll ensure that these resources pay for themselves over time. And you may save on initial capital investments.

> *Example:* In its new Shanghai carpet factory, Interface redesigned their process for pumping liquids by using fatter-than-usual pipes, which created less friction than thin pipes do. The move cut power requirements by 92%. The new system also cost less to build, involved no new technology, and worked better than traditional systems in all respects.

Imitate Biological Production Models

In nature, nothing goes to waste. Ensure that every output of your manufacturing processes is composted into useful natural resources or recycled for further production. You'll preserve ecosystems while eliminating the cost of waste disposal.

> *Example:* Interface invented a new floor-covering material, Solenium, which can be completely recycled into the identical floor product, reducing landfill waste. Solenium lasts four times longer and uses 40% less material than ordinary carpets. It's toxin-free and stainproof, resists mildew growth, and is easily cleaned with water. Between 1994 and 1998,

of capital—the "natural capital" of ecosystem services—were properly valued. The journey to natural capitalism involves four major shifts in business practices, all vitally interlinked:

- **Dramatically increase the productivity of natural resources.** Reducing the wasteful and destructive flow of resources from depletion to pollution

Interface's revenues rose by $200 million. Of those revenues, $67 million has been attributed to the company's decreased waste.

Change Your Business Model

Your customers don't necessarily need to *own* your products. Often they merely need to be able to *use* them. Therefore, consider shifting your business model from selling products to providing services.

Example: Interface realized clients want to walk on and look at carpets—not necessarily own them. So it transformed itself from a company that sells carpets into one that provides floor-covering services. It leases its service for a monthly fee, taking responsibility for keeping its carpets clean and replacing worn carpet tiles. This business model vastly reduces the amount

of carpeting sent to landfills. And it improves customers' productivity by eliminating the need to close offices and remove furniture to replace entire carpets.

Reinvest in Natural Capital

Reinvest in restoring, sustaining, and expanding your natural habitat and biological resource base. You'll gain a public reputation for environmental responsibility—which translates into profitability.

Example: Engineering company Living Technologies has developed a system that uses linked tanks of bacteria, algae, and plants to turn sewage into clean water. Its approach yields cleaner water at a reduced cost, with no toxicity or odor (making it compatible with the company's residential neighborhood).

represents a major business opportunity. Through fundamental changes in both production design and technology, farsighted companies are developing ways to make natural resources—energy, minerals, water, forests—stretch five, ten, even 100 times further than they do today. These major resource savings often yield higher profits than

small resource savings do—or even saving no resources at all would—and not only pay for themselves over time but in many cases reduce initial
capital investments.

- **Shift to biologically inspired production models.**
Natural capitalism seeks not merely to reduce
waste but to eliminate the very concept of waste.
In closed-loop production systems, modeled on
nature's designs, every output either is returned
harmlessly to the ecosystem as a nutrient, like
compost, or becomes an input for manufacturing
another product. Such systems can often be designed to eliminate the use of toxic materials,
which can hamper nature's ability to reprocess
materials.

- **Move to a solutions-based business model.** The business model of traditional manufacturing rests on
the sale of goods. In the new model, value is instead delivered as a flow of services—providing
illumination, for example, rather than selling
lightbulbs. This model entails a new perception of
value, a move from the acquisition of goods as a
measure of affluence to one where well-being is
measured by the continuous satisfaction of
changing expectations for quality, utility, and
performance. The new relationship aligns the
interests of providers and customers in ways that
reward them for implementing the first two innovations of natural capitalism—resource productivity and closed-loop manufacturing.

- **Reinvest in natural capital.** Ultimately, business must restore, sustain, and expand the planet's ecosystems so that they can produce their vital services and biological resources even more abundantly. Pressures to do so are mounting as human needs expand, the costs engendered by deteriorating ecosystems rise, and the environmental awareness of consumers increases. Fortunately, these pressures all create business value.

Natural capitalism is not motivated by a current scarcity of natural resources. Indeed, although many biological resources, like fish, are becoming scarce, most mined resources, such as copper and oil, seem ever more abundant. Indices of average commodity prices are at 28-year lows, thanks partly to powerful extractive technologies, which are often subsidized and whose damage to natural capital remains unaccounted for. Yet even despite these artificially low prices, using resources manyfold more productively can now be so profitable that pioneering companies—large and small—have already embarked on the journey toward natural capitalism.[1]

Still the question arises—if large resource savings are available and profitable, why haven't they all been captured already? The answer is simple: Scores of common practices in both the private and public sectors systematically reward companies for wasting natural resources and penalize them for boosting resource productivity. For example, most companies expense their consumption of raw materials through the income statement but pass resource-saving investment through the balance sheet. That distortion makes it more tax efficient to waste fuel than to invest in improving fuel efficiency. In short, even though the road seems clear, the compass that companies use to direct their journey is broken. Later we'll look in more detail at some of the obstacles to resource productivity—and some of the important business opportunities they reveal. But first, let's map the route toward natural capitalism.

Dramatically Increase the Productivity of Natural Resources

In the first stage of a company's journey toward natural capitalism, it strives to wring out the waste of energy, water, materials, and other resources throughout its production systems and other operations. There are two main ways companies can do this at a profit. First, they can adopt a fresh approach to design that considers industrial systems as a whole rather than part by part. Second, companies can replace old industrial technologies with new ones, particularly with those based on natural processes and materials.

Implementing Whole-System Design

Inventor Edwin Land once remarked that "people who seem to have had a new idea have often simply stopped having an old idea." This is particularly true when designing for resource savings. The old idea is one of diminishing returns—the greater the resource saving, the higher the cost. But that old idea is giving way to the new idea that bigger savings can cost less—that saving a large fraction of resources can actually cost less than saving a small fraction of resources. This is the concept of expanding returns, and it governs much of the revolutionary thinking behind whole-system design. Lean manufacturing is an example of whole-system thinking that has helped many companies dramatically reduce such forms of waste as lead times, defect rates, and inventory. Applying whole-system thinking to the productivity of natural resources can achieve even more.

Consider Interface, a leading maker of materials for commercial interiors. In its new Shanghai carpet factory, a liquid had to be circulated through a standard pumping loop similar to those used in nearly all industries. A top European company designed the system to use pumps requiring a total of 95 horsepower. But before construction began, Interface's engineer, Jan Schilham, realized that two embarrassingly simple design changes would cut that power requirement to only seven horsepower—a 92% reduction. His redesigned system cost less to build, involved no new technology, and worked better in all respects.

What two design changes achieved this 12-fold saving in pumping power? First, Schilham chose fatter-than-usual pipes, which create much less friction than thin pipes do and therefore need far less pumping energy. The original designer had chosen thin pipes because, according to the textbook method, the extra cost of fatter ones wouldn't be justified by the pumping energy that they would save. This standard design trade-off optimizes the pipes by themselves but "pessimizes" the larger system. Schilham optimized the *whole* system by counting not only the higher capital cost of the fatter pipes but also the *lower* capital cost of the smaller pumping equipment that would be needed. The pumps, motors, motor controls, and electrical components could all be much smaller because there'd be less friction to overcome. Capital cost would fall far more for the smaller equipment than it would rise for the fatter pipe. Choosing big pipes and small pumps—rather than small pipes and big pumps—would therefore make the whole system cost less to build, even before counting its future energy savings.

Schilham's second innovation was to reduce the friction even more by making the pipes short and straight rather than long and crooked. He did this by laying out the pipes first, *then* positioning the various tanks, boilers, and other equipment that they connected. Designers normally locate the production equipment in arbitrary positions and then have a pipe fitter connect everything. Awkward placement forces the pipes to make numerous bends that greatly increase friction. The pipe fitters don't mind: They're paid by the hour, they profit from the extra pipes and fittings, and they don't pay for the oversized pumps or inflated electric bills. In addition to reducing those four kinds of costs, Schilham's short, straight pipes were easier to insulate, saving an extra 70 kilowatts of heat loss and repaying the insulation's cost in three months.

This small example has big implications for two reasons. First, pumping is the largest application of motors, and motors use three-quarters of all industrial electricity. Second, the lessons are very widely relevant. Interface's pumping loop shows how simple changes in design mentality can yield huge resource savings and returns on investment. This isn't rocket science; often it's just a rediscovery of good Victorian engineering principles that have been lost because of specialization.

Whole-system thinking can help managers find small changes that lead to big savings that are cheap, free, or even better than free (because they make the whole system cheaper to build). They can do this because often the right investment in one part of the system can produce multiple benefits throughout the system. For example, companies would gain 18 distinct economic benefits—of which direct energy savings is only one—if they switched from ordinary motors to premium-efficiency motors or from ordinary lighting ballasts (the transformer-like boxes that control fluorescent lamps) to electronic ballasts that automatically dim the lamps to match available daylight. If everyone in America integrated these and other selected technologies into all existing motor and lighting systems in an optimal way, the nation's $220-billion-a-year electric bill would be cut in half. The after-tax return on investing in these changes would in most cases exceed 100% per year.

The profits from saving electricity could be increased even further if companies also incorporated the best off-the-shelf improvements into their building structure and their office, heating, cooling, and other equipment. Overall, such changes could cut national electricity consumption by at least 75% and produce returns of around

100% a year on the investments made. More important, because workers would be more comfortable, better able to see, and less fatigued by noise, their productivity and the quality of their output would rise. Eight recent case studies of people working in well-designed, energy-efficient buildings measured labor productivity gains of 6% to 16%. Since a typical office pays about 100 times as much for people as it does for energy, this increased productivity in people is worth about 6 to 16 times as much as eliminating the entire energy bill.

Energy-saving, productivity-enhancing improvements can often be achieved at even lower cost by piggybacking them onto the periodic renovations that all buildings and factories need. A recent proposal for real-locating the normal 20-year renovation budget for a standard 200,000-square-foot glass-clad office tower near Chicago shows the potential of whole-system design. The proposal suggested replacing the aging glazing system with a new kind of window that lets in nearly six times more daylight than the old sun-blocking glass units. The new windows would reduce the flow of heat and noise four times better than traditional windows do. So even though the glass costs slightly more, the overall cost of the renovation would be reduced because the windows would let in cool, glare-free daylight that, when combined with more efficient lighting and office equipment, would reduce the need for air-conditioning by 75%. Installing a fourfold more efficient, but fourfold smaller, air-conditioning system would cost $200,000 less than giving the old system its normal 20-year renovation. The $200,000 saved would, in turn, pay for the extra cost of the new windows and other improvements. This whole-system approach to renovation would not only save 75% of the building's total energy use, it would also greatly improve the building's comfort and marketability. Yet it would cost essentially the same as the normal renovation. There are about 100,000 20-year-old glass office towers in the United States that are ripe for such improvement.

Major gains in resource productivity require that the right steps be taken in the right order. Small changes made at the downstream end of a process often create far larger savings further upstream. In almost any industry that uses a pumping system, for example, saving one unit of liquid flow or friction in an exit pipe saves about ten units of fuel, cost, and pollution at the power station.

Of course, the original reduction in flow itself can bring direct benefits, which are often the reason changes are made in the first place. In the 1980s, while California's industry grew 30%, for example, its water use was cut by 30%, largely to avoid increased wastewater fees. But the resulting reduction in pumping energy (and the roughly tenfold larger saving in power-plant fuel and pollution) delivered bonus savings that were at the time largely unanticipated.

To see how downstream cuts in resource consumption can create huge savings upstream, consider how reducing the use of wood fiber disproportionately reduces the pressure to cut down forests. In round numbers, half of all harvested wood fiber is used for such structural products as lumber; the other half is used for paper and cardboard. In both cases, the biggest leverage comes from reducing the amount of the retail product used. If it takes, for example, three pounds of harvested trees to produce one pound of product, then saving one pound of product will save three pounds of trees—plus all the environmental damage avoided by not having to cut them down in the first place.

The easiest savings come from not using paper that's unwanted or unneeded. In an experiment at its Swiss headquarters, for example, Dow Europe cut office paper flow by about 30% in six weeks simply by discouraging unneeded information. For instance, mailing lists were eliminated and senders of memos got back receipts indicating whether each recipient had wanted the information. Taking those and other small steps, Dow was also able to increase labor productivity by a similar proportion because people could focus on what they really needed to read. Similarly, Danish hearing-aid maker Oticon saved upwards of 30% of its paper as a by-product of redesigning its business processes to produce better decisions faster. Setting the default on office printers and copiers to double-sided mode reduced AT&T's paper costs by about 15%. Recently developed copiers and printers can even strip off old toner and printer ink, permitting each sheet to be reused about ten times.

Further savings can come from using thinner but stronger and more opaque paper and from designing packaging more thoughtfully. In a 30-month effort at reducing such waste, Johnson & Johnson saved 2,750 tons of packaging, 1,600 tons of paper, $2.8 million, and at least 330 acres of forest annually. The downstream savings in paper use are multiplied by the savings further upstream, as less need for paper products (or less need for fiber to make each product) translates into less raw paper, less raw paper means less pulp, and less pulp requires fewer trees to be harvested from the forest. Recycling paper and substituting alternative fibers such as wheat straw will save even more.

Comparable savings can be achieved for the wood fiber used in structural products. Pacific Gas and Electric, for example, sponsored an innovative design developed by Davis Energy Group that used engineered wood products to reduce the amount of wood needed in a stud wall for a typical tract house by more than 70%. These walls were stronger, cheaper, more stable, and insulated twice as well. Using them enabled the designers to eliminate heating and cooling equipment in a climate where temperatures range from freezing to 113°F. Eliminating the equipment made the whole house much less expensive both to build and to run while still maintaining high levels of comfort. Taken together, these and many other savings in the paper and construction industries could make our use of wood fiber so much more productive that, in principle, the entire world's present wood fiber needs could probably be met by an intensive tree farm about the size of Iowa.

Adopting Innovative Technologies

Implementing whole-system design goes hand in hand with introducing alternative, environmentally friendly technologies. Many of these are already available and profitable but not widely known. Some, like the "designer catalysts" that are transforming the chemical industry, are already runaway successes. Others are still making their way to market, delayed by cultural rather than by economic or technical barriers.

The automobile industry is particularly ripe for technological change. After a century of development, motorcar technology is showing signs of age. Only 1% of the energy consumed by today's cars is actually used to move the driver: Only 15% to 20% of the power generated by burning gasoline reaches the wheels (the rest is lost in the engine and drivetrain) and 95% of the resulting propulsion moves the car, not the driver. The industry's infrastructure is hugely expensive and inefficient. Its convergent products compete for narrow niches in saturated core markets at commodity-like prices. Auto making is capital intensive, and product cycles are long. It is profitable in good years but subject to large losses in bad years. Like the typewriter industry just before the advent of personal computers, it is vulnerable to displacement by something completely different.

Enter the Hypercar. Since 1993, when Rocky Mountain Institute placed this automotive concept in the public domain, several dozen current and potential auto manufacturers have committed billions of dollars to its development and commercialization. The Hypercar integrates the best existing technologies to reduce the consumption of fuel as much as 85% and the amount of materials used up to 90% by introducing four main innovations.

First, making the vehicle out of advanced polymer composites, chiefly carbon fiber, reduces its weight by two-thirds while maintaining crashworthiness. Second, aerodynamic design and better tires reduce air resistance by as much as 70% and rolling resistance by up to 80%. Together, these innovations save about two-thirds of the fuel. Third, 30% to 50% of the remaining fuel is saved by using a "hybrid-electric" drive. In such a system, the wheels are turned by electric motors whose power is made onboard by a small engine or turbine, or even more efficiently by a fuel cell. The fuel cell generates electricity directly by chemically combining stored hydrogen with oxygen, producing pure hot water as its only by-product. Interactions between the small, clean, efficient power source and the ultralight, low-drag auto body then further reduce the weight, cost, and complexity of both. Fourth, much of the traditional hardware—from transmissions and differentials to gauges and certain parts of the suspension—can be replaced by electronics controlled with highly integrated, customizable, and upgradable software.

These technologies make it feasible to manufacture pollution-free, high-performance cars, sport utilities, pickup trucks, and vans that get 80 to 200 miles per gallon (or its energy equivalent in other fuels). These improvements will not require any compromise in quality or utility. Fuel savings will not come from making the vehicles small, sluggish, unsafe, or unaffordable, nor will they depend on government fuel taxes, mandates, or subsidies. Rather, Hypercars will succeed for the same reason that people buy compact discs instead of phonograph records: The CD is a superior product that redefines market expectations. From the manufacturers' perspective, Hypercars will cut cycle times, capital needs, body part counts, and assembly effort and space by as much as tenfold. Early adopters will have a huge competitive advantage—which is why dozens of corporations, including most automakers, are now racing to bring Hypercar-like products to market.[2]

In the long term, the Hypercar will transform industries other than automobiles. It will displace about an eighth of the steel market directly and most of the rest eventually, as carbon fiber becomes far cheaper. Hypercars and their cousins could ultimately save as much oil as OPEC now sells. Indeed, oil may well become uncompetitive as a fuel long before it becomes scarce and costly. Similar challenges face the coal and electricity industries because the development of the Hypercar is likely to accelerate greatly the commercialization of inexpensive hydrogen fuel cells. These fuel cells will help shift power production from centralized coal-fired and nuclear power stations to networks of decentralized, small-scale generators. In fact, fuel cell–powered Hypercars could themselves be part of these networks. They'd be, in effect, 20-kilowatt power plants on wheels. Given that cars are left parked—that is, unused—more than 95% of the time, these Hypercars could be plugged into a grid and could then sell back enough electricity to repay as much as half the predicted cost of leasing them. A national Hypercar fleet could ultimately have five to ten times the generating capacity of the national electric grid.

As radical as it sounds, the Hypercar is not an isolated case. Similar ideas are emerging in such industries as chemicals, semiconductors, general manufacturing, transportation, water and wastewater treatment, agriculture, forestry, energy, real estate, and urban design. For example, the amount of carbon dioxide released for each microchip manufactured can be reduced almost 100-fold through improvements that are now profitable or soon will be.

Some of the most striking developments come from emulating nature's techniques. In her book, *Biomimicry*, Janine Benyus points out that spiders convert digested crickets and flies into silk that's as strong as Kevlar without the need for boiling sulfuric acid and high-temperature extruders. Using no furnaces, abalone can convert seawater into an inner shell twice as tough as our best ceramics. Trees turn sunlight, water, soil, and air into cellulose, a sugar stronger than nylon but one-fourth as dense. They then bind it into wood, a natural composite with a higher bending strength than concrete, aluminum alloy, or steel. We may never become as skillful as spiders, abalone, or trees, but smart designers are already realizing that nature's environmentally benign chemistry offers attractive alternatives to industrial brute force.

Whether through better design or through new technologies, reducing waste represents a vast business opportunity. The U.S. economy is not even 10% as energy efficient as the laws of physics allow. Just the energy thrown off as waste heat by U.S. power stations equals the total energy use of Japan. Materials efficiency is even worse: only about 1% of all the materials mobilized to serve America is actually made into products and still in use six months after sale. In every sector, there are opportunities for reducing the amount of resources that go into a production process, the steps required to run that process, and the amount of pollution generated and by-products discarded at the end. These all represent avoidable costs and hence profits to be won.

Redesign Production According to Biological Models

In the second stage on the journey to natural capitalism, companies use closed-loop manufacturing to create new products and processes that can totally prevent waste. This plus more efficient production processes could cut companies' long-term materials requirements by more than 90% in most sectors.

The central principle of closed-loop manufacturing, as architect Paul Bierman-Lytle of the engineering firm CH2M Hill puts it, is "waste equals food." Every output of manufacturing should be either composted into natural nutrients or remanufactured into technical nutrients—that is, it should be returned to the ecosystem or recycled for further production. Closed-loop production systems are designed to eliminate any materials that incur disposal costs, especially toxic ones, because the alternative—isolating them to prevent harm to natural systems—tends to be costly and risky. Indeed, meeting EPA and OSHA standards by eliminating harmful materials often makes a manufacturing process cost less than the hazardous process it replaced. Motorola, for example, formerly used chlorofluorocarbons for cleaning printed circuit boards after soldering. When

CFCs were outlawed because they destroy stratospheric ozone, Motorola at first explored such alternatives as orange-peel terpenes. But it turned out to be even cheaper—and to produce a better product—to redesign the whole soldering process so that it needed no cleaning operations or cleaning materials at all.

Closed-loop manufacturing is more than just a theory. The U.S. remanufacturing industry in 1996 reported revenues of $53 billion—more than consumer-durables manufacturing (appliances; furniture; audio, video, farm, and garden equipment). Xerox, whose bottom line has swelled by $700 million from remanufacturing, expects to save another $1 billion just by remanufacturing its new, entirely reusable or recyclable line of "green" photocopiers. What's more, policy makers in some countries are already taking steps to encourage industry to think along these lines. German law, for example, makes many manufacturers responsible for their products forever, and Japan is following suit.

Combining closed-loop manufacturing with resource efficiency is especially powerful. DuPont, for example, gets much of its polyester industrial film back from customers after they use it and recycles it into new film. DuPont also makes its polyester film ever stronger and thinner so it uses less material and costs less to make. Yet because the film performs better, customers are willing to pay more for it. As DuPont chairman Jack Krol noted in 1997, "Our ability to continually improve the inherent properties [of our films] enables this process [of developing more productive materials, at lower cost, and higher profits] to go on indefinitely."

Interface is leading the way to this next frontier of industrial ecology. While its competitors are "down cycling" nylon-and-PVC-based carpet into less valuable carpet backing, Interface has invented a new floor-covering material called Solenium, which can be completely remanufactured into identical new product. This fundamental innovation emerged from a clean-sheet redesign. Executives at Interface didn't ask how they could sell more carpet of the familiar kind; they asked how they could create a dream product that would best meet their customers' needs while protecting and nourishing natural capital.

Solenium lasts four times longer and uses 40% less material than ordinary carpets—an 86% reduction in materials intensity. What's more, Solenium is free of chlorine and other toxic materials, is virtually stain-proof, doesn't grow mildew, can easily be cleaned with water, and offers aesthetic advantages over traditional carpets. It's so superior in every respect that Interface doesn't market it as an environmental product—just a better one.

Solenium is only one part of Interface's drive to eliminate every form of waste. Chairman Ray C. Anderson defines waste as "any measurable input that does not produce customer value," and he considers all inputs to be waste until shown otherwise. Between 1994 and 1998, this zero-waste approach led to a systematic treasure hunt that helped to keep resource inputs constant while revenues rose by $200 million. Indeed, $67 million of the revenue increase can be directly attributed to the company's 60% reduction in landfill waste.

Subsequently, president Charlie Eitel expanded the definition of waste to include all fossil fuel inputs, and now many customers are eager to buy products from the company's recently opened solar-powered carpet factory. Interface's green strategy has not only won plaudits from environmentalists, it has also proved a remarkably successful business strategy. Between 1993 and 1998, revenue has more than doubled, profits have more than tripled, and the number of employees has increased by 73%.

Change the Business Model

In addition to its drive to eliminate waste, Interface has made a fundamental shift in its business model—the third stage on the journey toward natural capitalism. The company has realized that clients want to walk on and look at carpets—but not necessarily to own them. Traditionally, broadloom carpets in office buildings are replaced every decade because some portions look worn out. When that happens, companies suffer the disruption of shutting down their offices and removing their furniture. Billions of pounds of carpets are removed each year and sent to landfills, where they will last up to 20,000 years. To escape this unproductive and wasteful cycle, Interface is transforming itself from a company that sells and fits carpets into one that provides floor-covering services.

Under its Evergreen Lease, Interface no longer sells carpets but rather leases a floor-covering service for a monthly fee, accepting responsibility for keeping the carpet fresh and clean. Monthly inspections detect and replace worn carpet tiles. Since at most 20% of an area typically shows at least 80% of the wear, replacing only the worn parts reduces the consumption of carpeting material by about 80%. It also minimizes the disruption that customers experience—worn tiles are seldom found under furniture. Finally, for the customer, leasing carpets can provide a tax advantage by turning a capital expenditure into a tax-deductible expense. The result: The customer gets cheaper and better services that cost the supplier far less to produce. Indeed, the energy saved from not producing a whole new carpet is in itself enough to produce all the carpeting that the new business model requires. Taken together, the five-fold savings in carpeting material that Interface achieves through the Evergreen Lease and the seven-fold materials savings achieved through the use of Solenium deliver a stunning 35-fold reduction in the flow of materials needed to sustain a superior floor-covering service. Remanufacturing, and even making carpet initially from renewable materials, can then reduce the extraction of virgin resources essentially to the company's goal of zero.

Interface's shift to a service-leasing business reflects a fundamental change from the basic model of most manufacturing companies, which still look on their businesses as machines for producing and selling products. The more products sold, the better—at least for the company, if not always for the customer or the earth. But any model that wastes natural resources also wastes money. Ultimately, that model will be unable to compete with a service model that emphasizes solving problems and building long-term relationships with customers rather than making and selling products. The shift to what James Womack of the Lean Enterprise Institute calls a "solutions economy" will almost always improve customer value *and* providers' bottom lines because it aligns both parties' interests, offering rewards for doing more and better with less.

Interface is not alone. Elevator giant Schindler, for example, prefers leasing vertical transportation services to selling elevators because leasing lets it capture the savings from its elevators' lower energy and maintenance costs. Dow Chemical and Safety-Kleen prefer leasing dissolving services to selling solvents because they can reuse the same solvent scores of times, reducing costs. United Technologies' Carrier division, the world's largest manufacturer of air conditioners, is shifting its mission from selling air conditioners to leasing comfort. Making its air conditioners more durable and efficient may compromise future equipment sales, but it provides what customers want and will pay for— better comfort at lower cost. But Carrier is going even further. It's starting to team up with other companies to make buildings more efficient so that they need less air-conditioning, or even none at all, to yield the same level of comfort. Carrier will get paid to provide the agreed-upon level of comfort, however that's delivered. Higher profits will come from providing better solutions rather than from selling more equipment. Since comfort with little or no air-conditioning (via better building design) works better and costs less than comfort with copious air-conditioning, Carrier is smart to capture this opportunity itself before its competitors do. As they say at 3M: "We'd rather eat our *own* lunch, thank you."

The shift to a service business model promises benefits not just to participating businesses but to the entire economy as well. Womack points out that by helping customers reduce their need for capital goods such as carpets or elevators, and by rewarding suppliers for extending and maximizing asset values rather than for churning them, adoption of the service model will reduce the volatility in the turnover of capital goods that lies at the heart of the business cycle. That would significantly reduce the overall volatility of the world's economy. At present, the producers of capital goods face feast or famine because the buying decisions of households and corporations are extremely sensitive to fluctuating income. But in a continuous-flow-of-services economy, those swings would be greatly reduced, bringing a welcome stability to businesses. Excess capacity—another form of waste and source of risk—need no longer be retained for meeting peak demand. The result of adopting the new model would be an economy in which we grow and get richer by using less and become stronger by being leaner and more stable.

Reinvest in Natural Capital

The foundation of textbook capitalism is the prudent reinvestment of earnings in productive capital. Natural capitalists who have dramatically raised their resource productivity, closed their loops, and shifted to a solutions-based business model have one key task remaining. They must reinvest in restoring, sustaining, and expanding the most important form of capital—their own natural habitat and biological resource base.

This was not always so important. Until recently, business could ignore damage to the ecosystem because it didn't affect production and didn't increase costs. But that situation is changing. In 1998 alone, violent weather displaced 300 million people and caused upwards of $90 billion worth of damage, representing more weather-related destruction than was reported through the entire decade of the 1980s. The increase in damage is strongly linked to deforestation and climate change, factors that accelerate the frequency and severity of natural disasters and are the consequences of inefficient industrialization. If the flow of services from industrial systems is to be sustained or increased in the future for a growing population, the vital flow of services from living systems will have to be maintained or increased as well. Without reinvestment in natural capital, shortages of ecosystem services are likely to become the limiting factor to prosperity in the next century. When a manufacturer realizes that a supplier of key components is overextended and running behind on deliveries, it takes immediate action lest its own production lines come to a halt. The ecosystem is a supplier of key components for the life of the planet, and it is now falling behind on its orders.

Failure to protect and reinvest in natural capital can also hit a company's revenues indirectly. Many companies are discovering that public perceptions of environmental responsibility, or its lack thereof, affect sales. MacMillan Bloedel, targeted by environmental activists as an emblematic clear-cutter and chlorine user, lost 5% of its sales almost overnight when dropped as a U.K. supplier by Scott Paper and Kimberly-Clark. Numerous case studies show that companies leading the way in implementing changes that help protect the environment tend to gain disproportionate advantage, while companies perceived as irresponsible lose their franchise, their legitimacy, and their shirts. Even businesses that claim to be committed to the concept of sustainable development but whose strategy is seen as mistaken, like Monsanto, are encountering stiffening public resistance to their products. Not surprisingly, University of Oregon business professor Michael Russo, along with many other analysts, has found that a strong environmental rating is "a consistent predictor of profitability."

The pioneering corporations that have made reinvestments in natural capital are starting to see some interesting paybacks. The independent power producer AES, for example, has long pursued a policy of planting trees to offset the carbon emissions of its power plants. That ethical stance, once thought quixotic, now looks like a smart investment because a dozen brokers are now starting to create markets in carbon reduction. Similarly, certification by the Forest Stewardship Council of certain sustainably grown and harvested products has given Collins Pine the extra profit margins that enabled its U.S. manufacturing operations to survive brutal competition. Taking an even longer view, Swiss

Re and other European reinsurers are seeking to cut their storm-damage losses by pressing for international public policy to protect the climate and by investing in climate-safe technologies that also promise good profits. Yet most companies still do not realize that a vibrant ecological web underpins their survival and their business success. Enriching natural capital is not just a public good—it is vital to every company's longevity.

It turns out that changing industrial processes so that they actually replenish and magnify the stock of natural capital can prove especially profitable because nature does the production; people need to just step back and let life flourish. Industries that directly harvest living resources, such as forestry, farming, and fishing, offer the most suggestive examples. Here are three:

- Allan Savory of the Center for Holistic Management in Albuquerque, New Mexico, has redesigned cattle ranching to raise the carrying capacity of rangelands, which have often been degraded not by overgrazing but by undergrazing and grazing the wrong way. Savory's solution is to keep the cattle moving from place to place, grazing intensively but briefly at each site, so that they mimic the dense but constantly moving herds of native grazing animals that coevolved with grasslands. Thousands of ranchers are estimated to be applying this approach, improving both their range and their profits. This "management-intensive rotational grazing" method, long standard in New Zealand, yields such clearly superior returns that over 15% of Wisconsin's dairy farms have adopted it in the past few years.

- The California Rice Industry Association has discovered that letting nature's diversity flourish can be more profitable than forcing it to produce a single product. By flooding 150,000 to 200,000 acres of Sacramento valley rice fields—about 30% of California's rice-growing area—after harvest, farmers are able to create seasonal wetlands that support millions of wildfowl, replenish groundwater, improve fertility, and yield other valuable benefits. In addition, the farmers bale and sell the rice straw, whose high silica content—formerly an air-pollution hazard when the straw was burned— adds insect resistance and hence value as a construction material when it's resold instead.

- John Todd of Living Technologies in Burlington, Vermont, has used biological Living Machines— linked tanks of bacteria, algae, plants, and other organisms—to turn sewage into clean water. That not only yields cleaner water at a reduced cost, with no toxicity or odor, but it also produces commercially valuable flowers and makes the plant compatible with its residential neighborhood. A similar plant at the Ethel M Chocolates factory in Las Vegas, Nevada, not only handles difficult industrial wastes effectively but is showcased in its public tours.

Although such practices are still evolving, the broad lessons they teach are clear. In almost all climates, soils, and societies, working with nature is more productive than working against it. Reinvesting in nature allows farmers, fishermen, and forest managers to match or exceed the high yields and profits sustained by traditional input-intensive, chemically driven practices. Although much of mainstream business is still headed the other way, the profitability of sustainable, nature-emulating practices is already being proven. In the future, many industries that don't now consider themselves dependent on a biological resource base will become more so as they shift their raw materials and production processes more to biological ones. There is evidence that many business leaders are starting to think this way. The consulting firm Arthur D. Little surveyed a group of North American and European business leaders and found that 83% of them already believe that they can derive "real business value [from implementing a] sustainable-development approach to strategy and operations."

A Broken Compass?

If the road ahead is this clear, why are so many companies straying or falling by the wayside? We believe the reason is that the instruments companies use to set their targets, measure their performance, and hand out rewards are faulty. In other words, the markets are full of distortions and perverse incentives. Of the more than 60 specific forms of misdirection that we have identified,[3] the most obvious involve the ways companies allocate capital and the way governments set policy and

impose taxes. Merely correcting these defective practices would uncover huge opportunities for profit.

Consider how companies make purchasing decisions.
Decisions to buy small items are typically based on their
initial cost rather than their full life-cycle cost, a practice
that can add up to major wastage. Distribution transformers that supply electricity to buildings and factories,
for example, are a minor item at just $320 apiece, and
most companies try to save a quick buck by buying the
lowest-price models. Yet nearly all the nation's electricity
must flow through transformers, and using the cheaper
but less efficient models wastes $1 billion a year. Such ex-
amples are legion. Equipping standard new office-light-
ing circuits with fatter wire that reduces electrical
resistance could generate after-tax returns of 193% a
year. Instead, wire as thin as the National Electrical Code
permits is usually selected because it costs less up front.
But the code is meant only to prevent fires from over-
heated wiring, not to save money. Ironically, an electri-
cian who chooses fatter wire—thereby reducing
long-term electricity bills—doesn't get the job. After paying for the extra copper, he's no longer the low bidder.

Some companies do consider more than just the initial price in their purchasing decisions but still don't go
far enough. Most of them use a crude payback estimate
rather than more accurate metrics like discounted cash
flow. A few years ago, the median simple payback these
companies were demanding from energy efficiency was
1.9 years. That's equivalent to requiring an after-tax
return of around 71% per year—about six times the mar-
ginal cost of capital.

Most companies also miss major opportunities by treating their facilities costs as an overhead to be minimized, typically by laying off engineers, rather than as a profit center to be optimized—by using those engineers to save resources. Deficient measurement and accounting practices also prevent companies from allocating costs—and waste—with any accuracy. For example, only a few semiconductor plants worldwide regularly and accurately measure how much energy they're using to produce a unit of chilled water or clean air for their clean-room production facilities. That makes it hard for them to improve efficiency. In fact, in an effort to save time, semiconductor makers frequently build new plants as exact copies of previous ones—a design method nicknamed "infectious repetitis."

Many executives pay too little attention to saving resources because they are often a small percentage of total costs (energy costs run to about 2% in most industries). But those resource savings drop straight to the bottom line and so represent a far greater percentage of profits. Many executives also think they already "did" efficiency in the 1970s, when the oil shock forced them to rethink old habits. They're forgetting that with today's far better technologies, it's profitable to start all over again. Malden Mills, the Massachusetts maker of such products as Polartec, was already using "efficient" metal-halide lamps in the mid-1990s. But a recent warehouse retrofit reduced the energy used for lighting by another 93%, improved visibility, and paid for itself in 18 months.

The way people are rewarded often creates perverse incentives. Architects and engineers, for example, are traditionally compensated for what they spend, not for what they save. Even the striking economics of the retrofit design for the Chicago office tower described earlier wasn't incentive enough actually to implement it. The property was controlled by a leasing agent who earned a commission every time she leased space, so she didn't want to wait the few extra months needed to refit the building. Her decision to reject the efficiency-quadrupling renovation proved costly for both her and her client. The building was so uncomfortable and expensive to occupy that it didn't lease, so ultimately the owner had to unload it at a fire-sale price. Moreover, the new owner will for the next 20 years be deprived of the opportunity to save capital cost.

If corporate practices obscure the benefits of natural capitalism, government policy positively undermines it. In nearly every country on the planet, tax laws penalize what we want more of—jobs and income—while subsidizing what we want less of—resource depletion and pollution. In every state but Oregon, regulated utilities are rewarded for selling more energy, water, and other resources, and penalized for selling less, even if increased production would cost more than improved customer efficiency. In most of America's arid western states, use-it-or-lose-it water laws encourage inefficient water consumption. Additionally, in many towns, inefficient use of land is enforced through outdated regulations, such as guidelines for ultrawide suburban streets recommended by 1950s civil-defense planners to accommodate the heavy equipment needed to clear up rubble after a nuclear attack.

The costs of these perverse incentives are staggering: $300 billion in annual energy wasted in the United States, and $1 trillion already misallocated to unnecessary air-conditioning equipment and the power supplies to run it (about 40% of the nation's peak electric load). Across the entire economy, unneeded expenditures to subsidize, encourage, and try to remedy inefficiency and damage that should not have occurred in the first place probably account for most, if not all, of the GDP growth of the past two decades. Indeed, according to former World Bank economist Herman Daly and his colleague John Cobb (along with many other analysts), Americans are hardly better off than they were in 1980. But if the U.S. government and private industry could redirect the dollars currently earmarked for remedial costs toward reinvestment in natural and human capital, they could bring about a genuine improvement in the nation's welfare. Companies, too, are finding that wasting resources also means wasting money and people. These intertwined forms of waste have equally intertwined solutions. Firing the unproductive tons, gallons, and kilowatt-hours often makes it possible to keep the people, who will have more and better work to do.

Recognizing the Scarcity Shift

In the end, the real trouble with our economic compass is that it points in exactly the wrong direction. Most businesses are behaving as if people were still scarce and nature still abundant—the conditions that helped to fuel the first Industrial Revolution. At that time, people were relatively scarce compared with the present-day population. The rapid mechanization of the textile industries caused explosive economic growth that created labor shortages in the factory and the field. The Industrial Revolution, responding to those shortages and mechanizing one industry after another, made people a hundred times more productive than they had ever been.

The logic of economizing on the scarcest resource, because it limits progress, remains correct. But the pattern of scarcity is shifting: Now people aren't scarce but nature is. This shows up first in industries that depend directly on ecological health. Here, production is increasingly constrained by fish rather than by boats and nets, by forests rather than by chain saws, by fertile topsoil rather than by plows. Moreover, unlike the traditional factors of industrial production—capital and labor—the biological limiting factors cannot be substituted for one another. In the industrial system, we can easily exchange machinery for labor. But no technology or amount of money can substitute for a stable climate and a productive biosphere. Even proper pricing can't replace the priceless.

Natural capitalism addresses those problems by reintegrating ecological with economic goals. Because it is both necessary and profitable, it will subsume traditional industrialism within a new economy and a new paradigm of production, just as industrialism previously subsumed agrarianism. The companies that first make the changes we have described will have a competitive edge. Those that don't make that effort won't be a problem because ultimately they won't be around. In making that choice, as Henry Ford said, "Whether you believe you can, or whether you believe you can't, you're absolutely right."

Notes

1. Our book, *Natural Capitalism*, provides hundreds of examples of how companies of almost every type and size, often through modest shifts in business logic and practice, have dramatically improved their bottom lines.

2. Nonproprietary details are posted at www.hypercar.com.

3. Summarized in the report "Climate: Making Sense *and* Making Money," at www.rmi.org/images/other/Climate/C97-13_ClimateMSMM.pdf.

AMORY B. LOVINS is a cofounder and the chairman of Rocky Mountain Institute (RMI), a nonprofit resource policy center in Colorado. **L. HUNTER LOVINS** is a cofounder of RMI and the president of Natural Capitalism, a Colorado firm that helps organizations create sustainability strategies. **PAUL HAWKEN** is the founder and executive director of Natural Capital Institute, a research group based in California.

Originally published in May 1999. Reprint R0707P

Don't Tweak Your Supply Chain—Rethink It End to End

by Hau L. Lee

HONG KONG-BASED ESQUEL, one of the world's leading producers of premium cotton shirts, faced a quandary in the early 2000s. Apparel and retail customers such as Nike and Marks & Spencer had begun asking the company about its environmental and social performance. Its leaders anticipated scrutiny from other customers as well, since more of them were demanding that a greater portion of the cotton in their shirts be grown organically. But the crop required a lot of water and pesticides, especially in poor and rapidly developing countries, where Esquel's cotton was grown and processed.

Though Esquel's executives wanted to strengthen the company's already serious commitment to social and environmental sustainability, they realized they couldn't simply demand that the farmers who supplied extra-long-staple cotton just reduce their use of water, fertilizer, and pesticides. A mandate like that could be catastrophic for the farmers and their villages. Most of Esquel's cotton came from Xinjiang, an arid province in northwestern China that depends mainly on underground sources of water. The traditional method of irrigation there was to periodically flood the fields—an inefficient approach that created a perfect breeding ground for insects and diseases. Heavy pesticide use was a necessity.

Productivity was an issue, too: A switch to organic cotton could cause crop yields to drop by as much as 50%. Even though the climbing demand for organic cotton was likely to boost prices, Esquel couldn't expect them to rise enough to compensate farmers for the lower yields. Indeed, apparel companies and retailers had made it abundantly clear that they would not be willing to pay a big premium for clothes made with organic cotton.

Complicating matters even more, organic cotton fiber is weaker than that of conventional cotton and has different physical characteristics. It would need extra processing, leave a greater percentage of scrap during fabric manufacturing, and require chemicals and dyes more environmentally harmful and more expensive than those used on conventional cotton. All this would add to costs and cancel out some of organic cotton's green benefits.

How could the shirtmaker provide the products customers demanded, conduct environmentally and socially responsible business in China, and protect its own profit margins?

Idea in Brief

With the best of intentions, companies up and down supply chains experiment with isolated efforts to improve sustainability—only to encounter a long string of unanticipated consequences, often in the form of financial, social, or environmental costs. That's partly because most firms respond in a piecemeal way to pressure from customers, shareholders, boards, employees, governments, and NGOs. For instance, they demand that suppliers change their materials to environmentally friendly ones or move manufacturing closer to end markets to reduce emissions from transportation. And they tweak their own operations by using compact fluorescent lamps, recycling more of their materials, and so on. Lee's research shows that it's much more effective to take a holistic approach to sustainability and make broader structural changes, as shirt manufacturer Esquel, steelmaker Posco, and others have done. Such changes can include reinventing processes, developing new kinds of relationships with business partners, and even collaborating with competitors to achieve scale. Stakeholders increasingly hold corporations accountable for supply chain partners' actions, as we've learned from widely publicized recalls of tainted pet food and lead-laden toys. Clearly, sustainability is a competitive concern. The core managers overseeing your supply chain must own and tackle it as aggressively as they do cost, quality, speed, and dependability.

Companies up and down supply chains in numerous industries confront the same challenge: A well-intentioned individual action or demand aimed at making a business greener can create a long string of unanticipated consequences that collectively dwarf the benefits.

The mounting pressure to conduct business in a sustainable fashion comes from various stakeholders—customers, shareholders, boards, employees, governments, and NGOs—and most corporations respond in a reactive, piecemeal way. They demand that suppliers change their materials to environmentally friendly ones. They ask suppliers to move manufacturing operations closer to end markets to reduce transportation-related carbon footprints. And they tweak their own operations by replacing ordinary lightbulbs with compact fluorescent lamps, recycling more of their materials, refurbishing and reusing products, using more energy-efficient equipment, and so on.

I call these actions *substitutions:* swapping one material, vendor, location, production step, or mode of transportation for another. Although each change might seem worthwhile, such actions can, when you factor in the unintended consequences, end up raising financial, social, or environmental costs and lead to supply chains that are not, well, sustainable.

Instead, companies—throughout the supply chain, not just at the end—should take a holistic approach to sustainability and pursue broader structural changes than they typically do. These may include sweeping innovations in production processes, the development of fundamentally different relationships with business partners that can evolve into new service models, and even collaboration with multiple companies to create new industry structures.

This is one of the most important conclusions to emerge from an ongoing research project I've been leading at Stanford Graduate School of Business. During the past seven years, my colleagues and I have studied supply chains in seven industries: agriculture, apparel, automobiles, electronics, high tech, retail, and resources (such as mining, steel, and cement). In addition to Esquel, we've looked at Adidas, CEMEX, the European Recycling Platform, Flextronics, Hewlett-Packard, Li & Fung, Netafim, Nike, Posco, Rio Tinto Iron Ore, Safeway, Smart Car, Starbucks, Toyota, Wal-Mart, and others.

In particular, we have focused on environmental and social responsibility in developing markets. Such economies provide the biggest opportunities for improving the environment, but they also entail the biggest risks. The widely publicized recalls of tainted pet food and lead-laden toys and children's belts made in China and the suicides of workers at a contractor's electronics factory in Shenzhen have driven home the reality that stakeholders increasingly hold corporations accountable for their supply chain partners' actions. Given the tremendous environmental damage that the explosion in manufacturing is inflicting on China, companies that source from China should expect their suppliers' greenness—or lack thereof—to come under more-intense scrutiny.

Clearly, sustainability issues are adding complexity and risks to the already daunting challenge of managing global supply chains. This suggests that companies need to pursue structural change much earlier than most currently do. Actions taken by Esquel and Posco, the South Korean steelmaker, are good examples of what I mean by structural change.

Esquel

To manage the trade-offs among environmental sustainability, social responsibility, and business performance,

Esquel helped independent farms and those it owned in Xinjiang try sustainable-farming techniques. For example, it assisted them in adopting drip irrigation to decrease their water use and in establishing natural pest- and disease-control programs, such as breeding disease-resistant strains of cotton, to reduce reliance on pesticides. (The new variety of cotton plants also produced stronger fiber, resulting in less scrap during fabric manufacturing than conventional cotton did.)

Esquel also introduced different harvesting techniques. Previously, farmers used chemical defoliants to induce leaves to drop to the ground so that machines could easily collect the crop. The shirtmaker suggested handpicking instead. Even though that would be more laborious up front, it would make for a cleaner harvest, saving the need to remove dirt and impurities later and reducing waste.

In addition, Esquel changed its supplier-customer relationships with independent farmers to be more like partnerships. For example, to enable farmers to invest in the new techniques, it teamed up with Standard Chartered Bank to provide microfinancing. And to decrease their risks, it started to place orders for cotton when it was planted and guaranteed payment of whichever price turned out to be higher at harvest—a company-set minimum or the prevailing market price.

As a result of these efforts, the yields of the organic farms in Xinjiang that serve Esquel more than doubled from 2005 to 2007; today they are the highest of any kind of cotton farm in China. Farmers' income has increased by 30% since 2005. And at a time when demand for organic cotton around the world is soaring, Esquel has secured a dependable, major supply.

The company improved its own manufacturing, as well. It developed new processes for washing, ginning, and spinning organic cotton fiber; created dyes that employed greener chemicals than those used to color conventional cotton fiber; and reduced the use of other chemicals in fabric manufacturing.

Posco

In a bid to make its steelmaking process more environmentally friendly, Posco had for years undertaken a host of discrete initiatives to conserve and recycle water, reduce its energy consumption, and control pollution. For example, it introduced continuous casters that allowed newly made steel to be rolled into products before it had completely cooled, which cut energy consumption by about 10%. It developed water management and reuse techniques that enabled the company to produce a ton of steel with just 3.8 cubic meters of water. And it recycled nonferrous slag—a by-product of steelmaking—by selling it to companies that used it to make cement and other construction materials.

Posco's managers thought they were doing all they possibly could to be green. Then a challenge arose that made them think otherwise. China's voracious demand for steel caused global prices of high-grade iron ore to rise sharply in the 1990s and the early 2000s. Making matters worse, oil prices also shot up, significantly increasing the cost of shipping the ore from distant mines. These trends prompted Posco to join forces with its equipment supplier, Siemens VAI: The companies set out to create a radically new technology that would cut costs and carbon emissions by using cheaper, lower-quality iron ore from mines much closer to Posco's mills.

The Finex steelmaking process is the solution they came up with. It can use cheaper bituminous coal and common iron ore powder, eliminates the need for coking and for sintering, and, compared with conventional steelmaking, requires substantially less energy and produces much lower levels of greenhouse gases and other pollutants. It has reduced the costs of building a new steel mill by 6% to 17% and slashed the operating cost by 15%. Posco has used the technology successfully in Korea and has reached an agreement with the Indian government to build a Finex mill in Orissa.

Figuring out how to pursue structural change and manage the trade-offs may sound daunting, but it doesn't have to be. It can be tackled in a systematic fashion. In the rest of this article, I offer some guidelines and best practices.

Manage Sustainability as a Core Operational Issue

The only way companies can recognize and navigate trade-offs or conflicts in their supply chains is to treat sustainability as integral to operations. They should consider it alongside issues such as inventory, cycle time, quality, and the costs of materials, production, and logistics.

Rethinking Your Supply Chain End to End

Connect the Dots Between Your Own Operations

By coordinating across every stage of fabric and shirt production, the Chinese manufacturer Esquel cut energy consumption by 26.4% and water consumption by 33.7% in the past five years.

Reinvent Your Manufacturing Processes

Companies often don't think about radically changing their manufacturing processes in order to become greener, but that's what Posco and its supplier Siemens VAI did: They came up with a new way of making steel that not only cut energy use and pollutants but also slashed mill-building costs by up to 17% and operating costs by 15%.

Work with Your Suppliers' Suppliers

Sometimes the critical players in your supply chain are several layers away. Starbucks faced this challenge and decided to forge direct relationships with farmers. Now it gets 81% of its coffee beans from sustainable suppliers, up from 25% in 2005.

Link Up with Competitors

If you can't achieve scale on your own, think about joining forces with rivals, as Hewlett-Packard, Electrolux, Sony, and Braun did when they formed the European Recycling Platform. ERP has cut manufacturers' recycling and disposal costs by as much as 35% in countries where it operates.

Recognizing this, Nike has made its supply chain managers—rather than a separate corporate social responsibility group—accountable for identifying possible sustainability improvements, implementing them, and tracking their performance. For example, in China, where the company has about 150 contract factories, its supply chain managers regularly evaluate existing and potential contract manufacturers on operational, environmental, and social-compliance measures. As part of this exercise, the managers consult a database of polluters maintained by the nonprofit Institute of Public and Environmental Affairs (IPE)—something many multinational corporations fail to do, according to Ma Jun, IPE's founder. When working with suppliers to improve their operational performance, Nike also trains them to boost their environmental and social performance.

To do all this at your company, start by mapping internal supply chain operations. Identify where environmental and social-responsibility problems or opportunities lie. Evaluate alternative ways to make improvements that may require trade-offs between the two types of performance. As you weigh your options, consider their potential social impact. After you choose and implement initiatives, continually measure their performance to ensure that you've achieved the right balance of environmental, social, and conventional operational considerations.

With this kind of approach, Esquel greatly improved both its sustainability and its overall operational performance in its vertically integrated business, which includes cotton farms, spinning mills, weaving and knitting operations, and final assembly. Each area has reduced energy consumption through process improvements, recycling, and the construction of thermal power plants; increased use of organic cotton; and decreased use of chemicals in dyeing. These environmental initiatives have also led to operational improvements: less scrap, lower cost, more-stable production, and fewer production stoppages and late deliveries to customers.

Coordinate with Adjacent Operations

Often, an internal operation can achieve only limited sustainability improvements on its own. Its adoption of a new material, component, or technology may require changes in adjacent units. Conversely, customers' operations often constrain the extent to which you can modify your own. For example, if a customer requires you to deliver once a day, you may not be able to fill up a truck, even though partial truckloads waste energy.

Start coordinating efforts by identifying all the overlapping activities. Then, working with the other parties, explore improvements you could make together that would transcend what any of you could achieve on your own. Since your priorities may differ, the metrics to track progress will have to be comprehensive enough to cover the interests of all operations.

When Esquel applied this approach, it found that its individual operating units typically didn't work together to become greener and, as a result, had missed opportunities. For example, in fabric production, a softener and chemicals used to improve seam strength and prevent threads from slipping were added to give the fabric a standard feel. But some of these chemicals were going down the drain during the garment-washing process. In response, Esquel developed a new recipe that reduced the amount of softener and anti-slippage agents but achieved the same feel. The company saved more than 1 million RMB annually, and it significantly decreased the waste discharged during garment washing.

Supply chain partners need to collaborate even on seemingly mundane sustainability initiatives, as the U.S. supermarket chain Safeway discovered when it set out to reduce the carbon footprint of packaging materials for products it received from manufacturers. The company examined transportation conveyances (boxes, pallets, wrappings, and such) and assessed several alternatives, including different kinds of pallets and slip sheets. Quantifying the environmental impact of each with a widely used life cycle assessment tool, Safeway discovered that the delivery frequency, the routing to different distribution centers, and the mix of products on a truck had to be modified for each conveyance. The company then worked with key manufacturers such as Procter & Gamble, Kimberly-Clark, and General Mills to implement changes. Safeway and its partners had to agree on a comprehensive set of environmental measures and goals for tracking progress in reducing emissions, energy consumption, and solid waste produced, along with parameters for standard operating costs.

Examine the Extended Supply Chain

After you've sought opportunities with adjacent internal operations and direct customers and suppliers, don't stop. Turn your attention to your suppliers' suppliers and your customers' customers—the extended supply chain. It's a critical step, not just to identify more-ambitious structural changes that could generate even greater payoffs but also to better manage risks.

Mattel learned this the hard way in 2007, when the discovery of lead paint on its toys damaged the brand and forced the company to conduct an expensive recall. A Chinese governmental agency traced the paint's source to a third-tier supplier, which had sold a batch of leaded yellow pigment to a paint company and had provided fake certification that it did not contain lead. The paint company had then sold the paint to Lee Der Industrial Company, one of Mattel's longtime contract manufacturers. Ignorance about the extended supply chain had left Mattel vulnerable to a single glitch upstream.

To avoid Mattel's travails, map out the members of your broader supply network and zero in on sustainability-related risks and opportunities. Figure out which performance indicators must be monitored to ensure that all members meet agreed-upon standards and targets. For instance, it's clear that Mattel needs to fully see the detailed specifications of the materials in its toys (including the lead content of the paint), the level of quality control efforts, and the results of inspections throughout its extended supply chain. Augment your own audits by consulting government agencies and NGOs that keep tabs on companies' social and environmental performance.

Once you have identified the vulnerabilities in your extended supply chain, you can collaborate with members to make improvements. To prevent a recurrence of the lead paint fiasco, Mattel may have to work with its first- and second-tier suppliers to detect issues early and train third-tier suppliers to keep problems from occurring in the first place.

That said, engaging members of the broader supply network in this manner can be extremely challenging— especially if they are several tiers below you, located far away, and based in developing economies, where secrecy is often the norm. Many companies hesitate to share information about their operating and environmental performance with other members of the extended supply chain out of fear that it might be used against them in contract negotiations or get leaked to competitors or regulators. So, you typically will have to educate members about why transparency is needed and how the information will be used.

To make major structural changes, parties must align their incentives. This may involve altering payment schemes or using other types of incentives—for example, providing direct aid in the form of training or subsidies—so that all partners believe they will benefit from the collaboration. Such alignment is the key to the *sustainability* of the sustainability initiatives, as Wal-Mart discovered. In 2005, when Wal-Mart initially mobilized its massive supplier network to join the company on its journey to become more environmentally responsible, it set aggressive goals for its suppliers to reduce energy consumption and the negative environmental

Winning the Trust of Communities in Emerging Economies

BECAUSE PEOPLE IN THE developing world often fear being exploited by foreign companies, they may resist businesses' efforts to get them to adopt sustainable production methods. So firms should make it clear how the public will benefit from working with them.

Toward this end, the shirtmaker Esquel has undertaken a number of educational initiatives for rural communities. Through the Esquel–Y.L. Yang Education Foundation, it has financed the renovation of decrepit schools in the province of Xinjiang and donated small local libraries. Employee and company contributions have provided thousands of children with financial assistance for tutoring, workbooks, and other basics.

To teach the importance of conservation, Esquel created the Ecomobile Lab, a classroom on wheels that brings hands-on activities such as tree planting to remote areas. Since it was launched, in 2004, it has reached 146 schools and more than 138,000 students and teachers and has sponsored the planting of more than 22,000 trees.

---

impacts of their production processes. Concerned that these measures would increase their costs without necessarily improving their revenues from Wal-Mart, many small and midsize suppliers in China did little or nothing. So Wal-Mart tried to mitigate their risks and increase the benefits of participating: It invested in training, codeveloped delivery processes that would cut suppliers' costs and its own, and provided guarantees of the quantities it would purchase from suppliers in the medium term. The carrot approach worked. In a 2009 audit of more than 100 Chinese factories serving Wal-Mart, the nonprofit Business for Social Responsibility found that they had become 5% more energy efficient in the program's first year.

The Starbucks Coffee and Farmer Equity (CAFE) program is another good example. Given consumers' interest in environmentally friendly food products, Starbucks pursued the goal of making coffee greener by persuading growers to farm more sustainably. But the company had no direct interactions with farmers; it had traditionally purchased coffee from intermediaries such as farm cooperatives, food processors, exporters, and importers. Therefore, it needed to involve the players throughout its extended supply chain, including the coffee farmers, in the effort.

The CAFE program spells out guidelines to promote environmental and social responsibility throughout the coffee supply chain: farming and processing practices that protect soil and biological diversity and conserve water and energy; worker pay that meets or exceeds minimum wage levels where the farms are located; adequate health, safety, and living conditions for workers; prohibitions on child labor; and limits on agricultural chemicals. It also fosters transparency by requiring suppliers to document how much of the money Starbucks pays for coffee actually reaches the grower, often a small family farmer in Latin America, Africa, or Asia.

Suppliers are graded by independent certifiers who largely come from NGOs such as Rainforest Alliance and who follow Starbucks's criteria. A supplier must score above a certain threshold to be CAFE certified. Starbucks buys first from certified farmers and suppliers and pays premium prices to top scorers and those who show continual improvement. (In 2009, beans from such suppliers accounted for 81% of Starbucks's coffee purchases, up from 77% in 2008 and 25% in 2005.)

Through the CAFE program, Starbucks offers loans to farmers trying to achieve high scores and provides training and support to ones failing to do so. Those incentives have helped the company lock in high-quality suppliers that are environmentally and socially responsible. With less supplier churn, it has managed to lower its long-term procurement costs and reduce its supply chain risk. For the coffee farmers, CAFE ensures a steady market for beans that can be sold at premium prices. So growers in poor and developing countries are given a chance to earn more-stable incomes and to protect themselves from volatility in world coffee prices.

Look Beyond Your Enterprise's Networks

Sometimes sustainability challenges are too great for the supply chain of any one enterprise to tackle on its own. Take recycling. A single company may not have the scale to support efficient collection and processing. If that's the case, the best solution is working with others' supply chains—even those of competitors. When multiple supply chains use the same materials, consume the same resources, or face the same threats, collaboration may bring cost-efficient, innovative solutions.

Of course, it requires careful planning and execution. The companies in the supply chains should have some objectives and interests in common. They must be able to share resources (processing capacity, labor, or materials) to gain economies of scale. They will have to work out the business model—including whether to establish a new independent entity or a joint venture, or whether to outsource the work to a third party. Finally, the results of the collaboration must be transparent to the participants, who in turn must be willing to share the knowledge and experiences gained from it.

In the early 1990s, many European countries set up inefficient systems for collecting discarded computers, monitors, televisions, household appliances, and other electronic products; recycling as much as they could; and safely disposing of the rest. In each country, a state-owned company took care of everything and charged manufacturers for its costs.

The onerous charges prompted four corporations—Hewlett-Packard, Electrolux, Sony, and Braun—to come up with a better alternative. They formed a joint venture: the European Recycling Platform (ERP). Set up as an independent business in December 2002, ERP has collected and recycled electronic waste for 34 companies in 11 countries. Its pan-European reach allows it to achieve much greater economies of scale than individual state-owned companies can, and the competition has sparked ERP to implement lean processes and become superefficient.

For example, HP's cost of recycling a digital camera is just 1 or 2 euro cents in Austria, Germany, and Spain, where ERP operates, and 7 euro cents to €1.24 in five countries where state-owned companies still enjoy monopolies. Recycling a laptop computer costs HP 7 to 39 euro cents in the three competitive countries and 88 euro cents to €6 in the other five.

In places where ERP operates, manufacturers' recycling and disposal costs have fallen by 10% to 35%. ERP has steadily expanded the scope of the products it handles, and its members now include Apple, Dell, Microsoft, Nike, and Nokia.

Sustainability is no longer a secondary issue. It has become a competitive concern and should be handled accordingly. The core managers overseeing the supply chain, not a peripheral CSR group, must own and tackle it as aggressively as they do cost, quality, speed, and dependability. They must engage the entire supply chain as they seek breakthroughs and try to minimize risks. Companies that take such a holistic approach will steal a march on reactive competitors. They will be sustained.

HAU L. LEE is the Thoma Professor of Operations, Information, and Technology at Stanford Graduate School of Business.

Originally published in October 2010. Reprint R1010C

Timberland's CEO on Standing Up to 65,000 Angry Activists

by Jeff Swartz

YOU CAN TELL A LOT about how your day is going to unfold by the number of e-mails that are waiting for you. I'm a pretty early riser—4 AM most days—so I typically start out ahead of the game when it comes to e-mails. But on June 1, 2009, they kept coming, and coming, and coming.

The first one accused Timberland of supporting slave labor, destroying Amazon rain forests, and exacerbating global warming—all in the first sentence. The second was a repeat of the first, as was the next, and the next. I had a funny feeling it was going to be a long day.

The fan mail was from Greenpeace supporters reacting to a newly released Greenpeace report about deforestation in the Amazon. The gist of the report was (a) Brazilian cattle farmers are illegally clear-cutting

Amazon rain forests to create pastures, and (b) the leather from their cows might be winding up in shoes—including Timberland's. (A) plus (b) equals (c): New Hampshire-based bootmakers are desecrating the environment. Take them to task. And take us to task they did. The senders didn't threaten a boycott but said they were "concerned" and urged us to work with Greenpeace to find a "permanent global solution" to both deforestation and climate change.

As a CEO, I'm used to getting angry e-mails—most of them along the lines of "You support something I oppose; therefore you're an idiot." But these were different. Even though their text was a form letter pulled off the Greenpeace website, it was well written and informed. And it was coming from a potent activist organization, suggesting a problem I wasn't intimately familiar with. Even in my early-morning haze, I knew that was a bad combination.

Throw away the Monday morning to-do list—we've got us an issue here.

That morning our IT department set up a system to automatically reroute all the activist e-mails from my inbox to a separate folder—not so that I could avoid them (although it was nice to have my inbox back), but because we wanted to make sure each one got a response.

Next on the agenda was figuring out *how* to respond—not just to Greenpeace's allegations, but to the angry senders, who totaled 65,000 over the next few weeks. I figured if that many people were taking the time to send an e-mail, there must be at least half a million not

Idea in Brief

Swartz awoke on June 1, 2009, to find the first of what, over time, would amount to 65,000 angry e-mails accusing Timberland of destroying Amazon rain forests and exacerbating global warming. The senders were reacting to a Greenpeace report alleging that Brazilian cattle farmers were illegally clearcutting forests to create pastures, and leather from their cows might be winding up in Timberland's boots. Swartz and his team had to craft a response immediately: The brand's reputation was at stake. He realized that the underlying question—Where did Timberland's leather come from?—was legitimate, and that he didn't know the answer. The idea of tracing hides back from tannery to pasture was daunting, but he saw the issue as a battle for the hearts and minds of environmental activists. The company opened a dialogue with Greenpeace and worked with its Brazilian supplier to get the origin of its hides certified. Meanwhile, Swartz made sure that all those e-mails received replies. In the end, Timberland praised Greenpeace for bringing the issue to the industry's attention, and Greenpeace acknowledged that Timberland had taken a leadership position on it.

sending e-mails who were also pissed off. That's a big number. Our brand's reputation was at stake.

My first response to the e-mails was to be pretty angry myself. Of all the environmental problems Timberland has been actively committed to addressing, deforestation tops the list. We've planted a million trees in China; we host community regreening events in cities all over the world. Our logo is a tree, for crying out loud. How much more ridiculous could this campaign be? It would have been laughable—if not for the 65,000 Greenpeace supporters who were buying into the allegations and making clear their expectation that we'd come up with an acceptable solution. The "or else" was implied, but we've all seen videos and news articles about big corporate bullies that fall victim to Greenpeace's wrath. I didn't want Timberland to be painted as either a corporate bully or a victim.

The Origin of Hides

Some members of our team, justifiably, thought our primary goal should be to figure out how to end the conversation—meaning get the angry activists to go away. Only about 7% of our leather is sourced from Brazil, so it would have been relatively easy to find another source that didn't come with strings such as deforestation issues and Greenpeace reports attached. This option became more compelling as other companies, including some of our competitors, started issuing statements in which they vowed to immediately stop buying leather from the region in question. "Let's just do what they're doing and say 'We're out,'" some colleagues advised.

I'm a third-generation CEO. I'm not the first guy into a fight. But I'm also not one to take the politically correct, cut-and-run route when I think something is worth staying and talking about—in this case, the reputation of our business and a serious environmental issue.

As much as I didn't want to admit it, Greenpeace was asking a legitimate question: Where was our leather coming from? Second on the list of things I didn't want to admit was that we didn't know the answer. We—our company, our industry—had until then never been asked, or asked ourselves, that question. Sure, we cared whether the leather came from a cow, a goat, or a pig.

But where did the animal graze before it went to the slaughterhouse? I'm a bootmaker, not a cattle rancher. That's not a question that was keeping me up at night—at least not before that June.

The fact is, the origin of hides has never been easily traceable: They're treated as a waste product by slaughterhouses, which are mostly interested in the meat. In some parts of the world, hides are sold in batches of two or three by guys on the side of the road. They're not tracked the way other materials—pharmaceuticals, for example, and most food products—are. The lack of traceability in our materials supply chain is almost archaic. But the thought of tracing one hide back through the tannery to the slaughterhouse to the cow to the herd to the pasture to the land—multiplied by however many hides make up the 7% of our leather that is sourced in Brazil—is enough to make your head hurt.

I was willing to suffer the headache—and impose it on my team—because I thought Greenpeace had raised a good question and that there was value in trying to answer it. I also saw this issue as a battle for the hearts and minds of environmental activists—the ones who believe that private enterprise by definition sucks and the world would be better off if companies burned down. I wanted to confront that notion head-on, to convince them that if they *really* want to help the rain forest—to make a sustainable environmental impact—they need the help of companies like Timberland. I wanted them to know that it's possible to be a profitable global business and also be actively engaged in protecting the environment.

Frugality Drives Sustainability

To understand how we responded to Greenpeace, it helps to understand the role that stakeholders—and issues like the environment—play in how Timberland operates. It also helps to understand that activist groups like Greenpeace have a unique operating model of their own.

Our environmental sensibility stems from being a frugal Yankee outdoor company. In Timberland's first factory, my grandfather used to walk around picking up the bobbins that fell off the machines to reuse them; every time, he'd say, "That's a penny." Leather came wrapped in thick green paper, and instead of throwing the wrapper away, my grandfather would smooth it out and make patterns from it. He wasn't recycling to save trees—he was thinking about not having to pay for the stock to cut a pattern.

Today we do a variety of things to minimize our use of resources—because my grandfather's frugality runs deep, and because we'd rather leave a light footprint on the earth than a heavy one. Our efforts to be environmentally responsible—from powering our facilities with renewable energy to calculating the carbon footprint of our footwear—made Greenpeace's allegations hard to swallow. Furthermore, we actively participate in cross-brand collaborations to address industry issues, and we host stakeholder calls once a quarter so that anyone concerned about the impact of our business can share questions and criticisms with us. It's not always comfortable to be bumping elbows with our toughest competitors or to sit in the hot seat during those calls.

But we benefit from outside perspectives. That's another reason why Greenpeace's guerrilla tactics—accuse first and engage later—felt like such an affront.

For Greenpeace, guerrilla tactics are supremely effective—something I was naive about when all this began. There's no question the organization cares about saving rain forests, but it also cares about recruiting new members and collecting membership fees. Making headlines by attacking companies helps it do that.

If Greenpeace wanted to start a dialogue with the footwear industry about how our supply chain might be hurting rain forests, I strongly feel that someone there should have picked up the phone. The organization could have convened the industry's CEOs to talk about these issues and craft a solution—and then held a press conference where it took credit for getting us to address the problem. There isn't one executive in our industry who wouldn't have wanted to be at that press conference. But phone calls and press conferences aren't as sexy as an attack campaign and wouldn't have riled up Greenpeace's member base, which is part of what drives its revenue. So it came at us instead, leading us to waste a ton of energy fighting a goopy mess rather than making meaningful progress.

We called Greenpeace within a few hours of receiving the first e-mail, but it took days to get someone knowledgeable about the issue to come to the phone. While we waited for the organization to talk to us, our supplier tried to get some answers. To illustrate its claim that ranchers were illegally clear-cutting the Amazon forest, Greenpeace published pictures from Google Earth showing cows grazing in places that had been forest just a month before. In conversations with our supplier, we learned that it didn't actually know where ranchers were pasturing their cattle—so Greenpeace might be right. Hmm . . . not the answer I was hoping for.

My next question for the team: If our supplier didn't know where the cattle originated, could we start figuring

Timberland's financials

Despite falling revenues, Timberland's net income is on the rise.

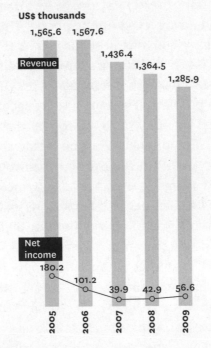

US$ thousands

Number of employees: 5,700
Headquarters: Spratham, NH
Source: Timberland

it out? Could we track where specific cows were graz-ing? Our engineers concluded that the task was arduous but not impossible; although there wasn't a system in place to capture and manage that data, there *could* be, given enough time and resources. What would make it impossible, they said, was if the companies further up the supply chain—the cattle ranchers and the slaugh-terhouses—were unwilling to go along with it.

It's called a supply chain for a reason: There are a lot of links—ranchers, slaughterhouses, tanneries. In the scheme of things in Brazil, we're a very small player with very little leverage. To its credit, Greenpeace understood this. So it didn't come after shoe companies only—it also targeted companies that buy beef, includ-ing Wal-Mart and other grocery chains. It applied pres-sure to Brazilian politicians, who turned to Brazilian law enforcement, which began going after the ranchers who were breaking the law. Greenpeace effectively brought a coalition of pressure against every link in the chain simultaneously—a powerful tactic, and one it knew would work.

Our supplier had little choice but to take this seri-ously: All its customers were asking the same hard questions at the same time. We didn't have to threaten to cancel our contracts—the threat was implicit. The supplier knew it was going to have to step up.

Crafting a Response

Dealing with the supply chain would take weeks, if not longer—but in the meantime, we had 65,000 love notes

Finding the Right Tone

WHEN TIMBERLAND FACED an implied boycott threat from Greenpeace activists, it attacked the problem on two fronts: working with its Brazilian supplier to ensure that its practices weren't hurting the environment, and communicating with the Greenpeace e-mailers respectfully and transparently about its efforts to be part of a collaborative solution. Below are edited excerpts showing how the company's response evolved during the course of the campaign.

June 1

On the morning of June 1, 2009, the e-mails began flowing into CEO Jeff Swartz's inbox:

> Dear Mr. Swartz,
>   I am concerned that, given your company's dependence on leather to make shoes sold around the world, you may be supporting forest destruction, slave labor, the expulsion of indigenous groups within the Amazon Rainforest, and global climate change. . . .
>   As a consumer, I want to be confident that when I buy your shoes I have not contributed to Amazon destruction and climate change. . . . I look forward to hearing what steps you will take to help solve this problem.
>   Sincerely,

June 1–4

During the first four days of the campaign, Timberland replied with a lengthy, somewhat defensive e-mail:

> Thank you for your inquiry. . . . We take our environmental and community impact very seriously and work hard to do our part to preserve the planet by planting trees, reducing our contribution to global warming, developing environmentally-conscious products and encouraging civic action. . . . We do source some leather from Brazil, but we have been assured that the material is not sourced from deforested areas. . . . We share your concerns about deforestation . . . Timberland's tree planting initiative has resulted in more than one million trees planted across the globe since 2001. . . . We plan to plant another million trees by the end of 2011. . . .

June 5

Starting on the fifth day, Timberland decided a less-is-more approach might be more effective:

> Thank you for your inquiry. . . . Timberland is committed to minimizing the environmental impact of our business operations. We're interested in engaging with Greenpeace and others in our industry about this situation. . . .

July 24

After striking an agreement with Greenpeace, Timberland crafted a new message on July 24:

> . . . For more than 20 years, Timberland's approach to supplier relationships has been one of active, mutual engagement . . . we have an unflinching commitment to work with our value chain to address failures. . . . Our principles apply in the Amazon, and so we are working closely with our supplier in Brazil to ensure they have an action plan in place that addresses their commitment to an immediate moratorium on deforestation in the Amazon Biome, and of course refraining from sourcing products from indigenous or protected lands or entities that engage in slave labor. . . .

October 30

On October 30 Timberland sent a lengthy e-mail update signed by CEO Jeff Swartz to everyone who'd contacted the company on this issue:

> . . . Three months later, real progress to report. . . . Last month [our supplier] publicly announced their official Amazon cattle moratorium . . . and is working aggressively to meet traceability targets to ensure the origin of all the cattle they source is acceptable and not contributing to Amazon deforestation. . . . For its part, Greenpeace has done an outstanding job gathering data, creating a complete and compelling case for the issue, and mobilizing its tens of thousands of supporters. . . . Their effort has driven change into the system. We applaud their activism. . . .

to respond to. Bill Clinton likes to say that when it comes to winning votes, you need to consider two kinds of people: the Nos and the Maybes. Now, the Nos are against you all the way; you can't win their votes, so you shouldn't waste time trying. Every election, he says, is won or lost on the Maybes—they're your fighting chance. Even though we had no way of differentiating Nos from Maybes, given the cookie-cutter e-mail, we knew we had to craft a response that had the best possible chance of winning the Maybes (provided there were any in the bunch)—those who might, just might, see that we were trying to do the right thing.

Our response ended up evolving over time (see the sidebar "Finding the Right Tone"). Writing an e-mail response may seem like a no-brainer, but we worked really hard to get it right. For instance, if an e-mail had come from an Italian internet address—even if the message was in English—we replied in Italian. And we watched how many senders replied. We never expected that everyone would write back and say, "Wow, we never realized you were great guys!" but we did hope to hear from activists who appreciated our response. And some of them did.

By July, we'd begun to make progress in working with our supplier and in consulting with our competitors and with Greenpeace. Although Greenpeace had hoped that we'd simply come out with a high-level statement agreeing with its position, we wanted to really understand the problem—and to make sure our supplier had a system in place that could be implemented and sustained.

On July 22, Nike announced that it would require its Brazilian leather suppliers to certify in writing that their hides hadn't come from deforested areas. Now, Nike is huge—a much bigger player than we are in terms of leather sourcing—and its suppliers would have to start mapping and tracking ranches all over the country. A few days later—seven weeks after the e-mail onslaught began—we reached a similar agreement with our supplier.

Implementing the agreement has been just as hard as we expected—even harder. Our leather supplier was acquired by a larger company last fall, which has predictably slowed things down. But our supplier has committed to certifying, in short order, that the hides it buys from large cattle ranches aren't coming from deforested areas—and to having smaller ranches mapped by 2011.

At the end of July 2009 we issued a statement praising Greenpeace for bringing the matter to the industry's attention, and it was able to declare victory. In return, it issued a statement saying that Timberland had taken a leadership position on the issue, which was as gratifying as praise from an organization that has painfully put you through the paces can be.

Here are some things I learned from the experience:

When angry activists come at you, don't stand there with your arms folded and your mind closed. You may not agree with their tactics, but they may be asking legitimate questions you should have been asking yourself. And if you can find at least one common goal—in this case, a solution to deforestation—you've also found at least one reason for working *with* each other, not against.

On the other hand, don't greet them naively with open arms. For every common goal, half a dozen personal agendas are in play. Greenpeace's include selling membership subscriptions as well as saving the world. If that weren't true, the organization would be making more phone calls and fewer sexy headlines.

In times of tension, watch and listen. That's when you learn just how committed you are to your principles—and how committed your team and your partners and even your competitors are to theirs.

Did any of this make a difference for the issue of deforestation in Brazil? The jury's still out and probably will be for a while. But I believe there's real value in the outcomes we've already seen and in the lessons I'll take with me as I continue to work to make Timberland a more responsible and sustainable organization—the same path I was on before the first e-mail came in, and the same path I'll be on tomorrow.

JEFF SWARTZ is the president and CEO of Timberland.

Originally published in September 2010. Reprint R1009A

Competitive Advantage on a Warming Planet

by Jonathan Lash and Fred Wellington

WHETHER YOU'RE IN A TRADITIONAL smokestack industry or a "clean" business like investment banking, your company will increasingly feel the effects of climate change. Even people skeptical of the dangers of global warming are recognizing that simply because so many others are concerned, the phenomenon has wide-ranging implications.

Investors already are discounting share prices of companies poorly positioned to compete in a warming world. Many businesses face higher raw material and energy costs as governments around the globe increasingly enact policies placing a cost on emissions. Consumers are taking into account a company's environmental record when making purchasing decisions. There's a burgeoning market in greenhouse gas emission allowances (the so-called carbon market), with annual trading in these assets valued at tens of billions of dollars. Even in the United States, which has lagged the rest of the developed world in the regulation of greenhouse gas emissions, the debate is rapidly shifting from whether climate change legislation should be enacted to when and in what form.

Companies that manage and mitigate their exposure to climate-change risks while seeking new opportunities for profit will generate a competitive advantage over rivals in a carbon-constrained future. We offer here a guide for identifying the ways in which climate change can affect your business and for creating a strategy that will help you manage the risks and pursue the opportunities. We cite examples of very different companies—from Caterpillar to Wal-Mart to Goldman Sachs—that are responding to the various forces unleashed by the growing awareness among business leaders and consumers of the importance of climate change. Our message: It's not enough to do something; you have to do it better—and more quickly—than your competitors.

The Effects of Climate Change on the Planet

Let us stop here for a second and state our belief that climate change does in fact pose a serious problem for the world. The buildup of greenhouse gases in the atmosphere is changing the earth's climate at a rate unprecedented in history. The year 2005 was the warmest on record, and the ten warmest years have all occurred since 1980. Ice in the Arctic, the Antarctic, and Greenland is melting, and virtually all of the world's glaciers are shrinking.

Idea in Brief

Global warming is affecting your business, no matter what industry you're in. You face numerous climate-change risks—including tough emission-reduction legislation, damaging backlash from environmentally concerned consumers, and weather-related damage to physical assets. Consumers are increasingly taking your environmental record into account when they make purchasing decisions. And investors are already discounting share prices of firms poorly positioned to compete in a carbon-constrained world.

But the risks of climate change also offer new sources of competitive advantage, say Lash and Wellington. How to seize those opportunities? First, measure your firm's contribution to global warming. Then assess your climate-related risks *and* opportunities. Reinvent your business—before rivals do—to mitigate those risks *and* seize the opportunities.

GE, for instance, launched Ecomagination—a set of clean technologies serving the transportation, energy, water, and consumer product sectors. Revenues from Ecomagination reached $8.5 billion in 2005, with orders and commitments nearly doubling to $17 billion.

Numerous studies suggest that the warming of the earth's oceans has resulted in more-powerful tropical storms, which generate their energy from warm ocean waters. For example, a U.S. government study released in May 2006 found that the warming of the tropical North Atlantic will contribute to more and stronger hurricanes. In fact, global data show that storms, droughts, and other weather-related disasters are growing more severe and more frequent.

These observed effects are the result of a roughly one-degree-Fahrenheit warming of the planet, an increase

Idea in Practice

Lash and Wellington recommend this four-step process for mitigating climate-related risks and seizing new opportunities for competitive advantage.

Step 1: Quantify Your Carbon "Footprint"

Using available reporting standards (such as the Greenhouse Gas Protocol), prepare an inventory that provides a true and fair account of your company's greenhouse gas emissions. Differentiate between direct (such as smokestack) emissions and indirect emissions (for example, those resulting from your firm's energy consumption and travel).

By quantifying your carbon "footprint," you signal to investors, customers, and employees your recognition that climate change is a crucial issue. And you begin gaining a broad view of the risks and opportunities presented by a carbon-constrained economy.

Step 2: Assess Your Carbon-Related Risks and Opportunities

Consider how the following risks could hurt—or present opportunities to help—your business:

- Regulatory—mandatory emissions-reduction legislation

- Supply chain—suppliers' passing their higher carbon-related costs to you

- Product and technology—rivals' developing climate-friendly offerings before you do

- Litigation—lawsuits charging you with negligence, public nuisance, or trespass

- Reputation—destructive consumer or shareholder backlash

---

that would accelerate under current emission trends, thereby increasing the pace of physical and biological changes. (See the sidebar "How Much Warmer Will It Get?") Half of the fossil fuels ever burned have been used since the end of World War II, and emissions

- Physical—damage to your assets through drought, floods, and storms

Example: Forest products company Weyerhauser could ask itself questions such as: "Will milder winters spur wood-beetle populations, damaging trees? Could climate change affect demand for our products, if customers require more energy efficient building materials—or increasingly choose wood over other materials?"

Step 3: Adapt Your Business

Based on your assessment of how climate change could affect your company, develop and implement strategies for reducing energy consumption and carbon emissions. And consider how you might reinvent parts of your business to seize new opportunities.

Example: Caterpillar is making its already relatively low emission diesel engines even more efficient. It is also building a new business: making particulate filter systems that can be retrofitted on its own and other manufacturers' engines. In addition, it's studying engines that run on bio-fuels.

Step 4: Do It Better Than Rivals

"Doing well by doing good" isn't enough: You have to beat rivals at reducing your exposure to climate-related risk and finding business opportunities within those risks.

Example: Honda and Toyota have bested competitors (including GM, DaimlerChrysler, and BMW) by making their fleets more fuel efficient than most rivals' *and* taking the lead in commercializing hybrid vehicles.

continue to rise rapidly. In order to halt the buildup of greenhouse gases in the earth's atmosphere, global emissions would have to stop growing at all in this decade and be reduced by an astonishing 60% from today's levels by 2050.

How Much Warmer Will It Get?

ACCORDING TO NASA, 2005 was the warmest year in over a century, and the ten warmest years have all occurred since 1980. The shrinking polar ice caps aren't the only apparent consequence: Storms, droughts, and other weather-related disasters—for example, epidemics, whose spread is correlated with temperature and moisture rates—are growing more severe and more frequent.

All that, and the planet has warmed only by roughly one degree Fahrenheit. Most climate models predict a three- to eight-degree rise in global average temperatures if atmospheric concentrations of greenhouse gases reach twice preindustrial levels, something that will happen by 2050 if current trends continue. All of those models show some risk (between 5% and 15%) that the temperature will rise significantly more than that. Furthermore, there is a risk of unknown magnitude that positive feedback mechanisms in the climate system—for instance, the release of methane from melting permafrost in northern Canada, which could contribute to global warming and further melting of the permafrost—will create sudden, nonlinear accelerations in warming.

Frequency of weather-related disasters

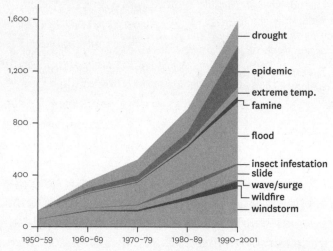

Source: Swiss Re

The consequences for the planet of inaction on climate change are becoming clear. But what exactly are the business implications?

The Effects of Climate Change on Your Company

Executives typically manage environmental risk as a threefold problem of regulatory compliance, potential liability from industrial accidents, and pollutant release mitigation. But climate change presents business risks that are different in kind because the impact is global, the problem is long-term, and the harm is essentially irreversible. Furthermore, U.S. government policies have offered companies operating in the United States little guidance as to how environmental policy may change in the future. Ignoring the financial and competitive consequences of climate change could lead a company to formulate an inaccurate risk profile.

While this obviously has been the case for utilities and energy-intensive industries like chemical manufacturing, it now holds true for most industries. In fact, the most important distinctions to be made when considering environmental risk assessment aren't between sectors but within sectors, where a company's climate-related risk mitigation and product strategies can create competitive advantage.

Government regulators aren't the only ones monitoring individual companies for inadequate climate-related practices. Big investors are beginning to demand more disclosure from companies. For example, the Carbon Disclosure Project, a coalition of institutional investors representing more than \$31 trillion in assets, annually requests information from large multinational companies about their climate-risk positioning. Its most recent report, released in 2006, showed a marked increase not only in the awareness of climate change on the part of the respondents but also in the best practices being developed to manage exposure to climate risk.

Similarly, investor coalitions are filing shareholder resolutions requesting more climate risk disclosure from companies. More than two dozen climate-related resolutions were filed with companies in the 2004 to 2005 period, triple the number from 2000 to 2001.

As Wal-Mart CEO Lee Scott told us, a corporate focus on reducing greenhouse gases as quickly as possible is a good business strategy: "It will save money for our customers, make us a more efficient business, and help position us to compete effectively in a carbon-constrained world."

The far-reaching effects of climate change on business become clearer when you start to think about the different kinds of risk—most of which can be transformed into opportunities—and how they could affect the value of your company.

Regulatory Risk

This is the most obvious area of impact, whether it takes the form of regulating emissions of the products you make (for example, automobile emission limits for carmakers) or of the manufacturing process you use in creating those products. Companies in much of the world are already subject to the Kyoto Protocol, which aims to reduce carbon dioxide and other greenhouse gases by requiring developed countries—and, by extension, companies operating within those countries—to limit greenhouse gas emissions.

To meet Kyoto targets, the European Union's Emissions Trading Scheme, for example, grants companies *allowances* that authorize them to emit certain amounts of specified greenhouse gases. If a company's emissions are higher than its allotted allowances, it has to buy additional allowances from other companies. If its emissions are lower than its allotment, it can sell its unneeded allowances on the market. Companies can earn *credits,* which also give the holder the right to emit certain amounts of gases, by investing in emissions abatement projects outside their own organizations and even countries—as when, say, a French company invests in a wind-powered electricity generation project in Brazil. These credits can either be used to offset companies' own emissions or be sold on the market.

Even in the United States, which withdrew from the Kyoto Protocol, various regional, state, and local government policies increasingly affect companies. Seven northeastern states have adopted an agreement to cap carbon emissions from utilities and establish a carbon-trading scheme. (See the sidebar "A U.S. Carbon Market.") California has enacted regulations requiring that from 2008 to 2016, greenhouse gas emissions from new cars be reduced by 30% and has passed legislation to reduce total emissions to 1990 levels by 2020. A 2007 executive order also requires a reduction in the carbon content in motor fuels. Twenty states require utilities to

A U.S. Carbon Market

THE EUROPEAN UNION'S MARKET that allows companies to buy and sell greenhouse gas emission credits granted under the Kyoto Protocol has received considerable attention. A similar kind of GHG market is beginning to form in the United States, at least on a regional basis, largely owing to the success of long-standing emissions trading systems for other kinds of air and water pollutants. The Regional Greenhouse Gas Initiative is a multistate government program aimed at reducing carbon dioxide emissions from power plants in the northeastern U.S. through a mix of emissions caps and the trading of emissions allowances. The initiative will govern GHG emissions from most electricity-generating units in the region that use more than 50% fossil fuel. Starting in 2009, and at the end of each three-year compliance period thereafter, each regulated source must own allowances equaling its aggregate carbon dioxide emissions during the period. Generating plants can buy, sell, bank, and trade allowances or purchase offset credits from other companies in ways that will keep their compliance costs as low as possible.

obtain a percentage of the power they sell from renewable sources, and more than 218 U.S. cities have adopted programs to reduce emissions.

The U.S. government seems increasingly likely to take some sort of action, possibly in the near future. One 30-country survey, conducted by GlobeScan, shows that 76% of Americans believe global warming is a serious problem, and half believe it is a very serious one. (All the other countries surveyed except Kenya and South Africa reported even greater concern on the part of residents.) Numerous emission-reduction bills have been introduced in the U.S. Congress, and, although federal legislation is still at least several years away, U.S. companies' investments in capital equipment—from power plants to new buildings—represent financial commitments to carbon dioxide emissions that may become very costly under future regulatory regimes.

For most businesses, a comprehensive federal policy concerning climate change is preferable to a patchwork of state and local regulations. Consequently, U.S. companies are beginning to shift their political position; more than 40 *Fortune* 500 companies have announced that they favor mandatory federal regulation of greenhouse gases. In January 2007, a group of leading companies, including Lehman Brothers, Alcoa, and Pacific Gas and Electric, called for rapid enactment of mandatory, economy-wide regulatory programs to support a 10% to 30% reduction of greenhouse gases over 15 years in the U.S. At a Senate hearing in 2006, representatives of companies such as General Electric, Duke Energy, and Exelon made the case that it was time to move forward with legislation. They would rather know the rules soon, they said, than be surprised by sudden political urgency.

By immediately initiating an assessment of how future legislation might affect them, companies can manage the regulatory risk and, crucially, gain an advantage over less prescient rivals.

Supply Chain Risk

As they assess their susceptibility to future regulations, companies should also evaluate the vulnerability of their suppliers, which could lead to higher component and energy costs as suppliers pass along increasing carbon-related costs to their customers. Auto manufacturing, for instance, relies heavily on suppliers of steel, aluminum, glass, rubber, and plastics, all of whom are likely to be seriously affected by emissions regulations or—as in the case of aluminum manufacturing, a big consumer of energy—by regulations on their suppliers' suppliers.

A company should also take into account the geographical distribution of its supplier network. Executives should be aware of how many of their suppliers operate in, say, the European Union, where regulatory structures are already in place. In addition, executives must be mindful that the other climate-related risks discussed here could affect not just their own companies but their suppliers as well.

Product and Technology Risk
Some companies will fare better than others in a carbon-constrained future, depending on their ability to identify ways to exploit new market opportunities for climate-friendly products and services.

For example, a technology for converting coal into energy (IGCC, or integrated gasification combined cycle), while currently more expensive than traditional methods used in pulverized-coal plants, can lower aggregate carbon emissions through better efficiency and possibly carbon dioxide capture and storage. In doing so, IGCC would reduce the significant costs that coal-fired plants would face under stricter emissions standards. Companies at the forefront of commercializing such technologies could see significant revenue growth as demand for low-carbon products increases.

Opportunities are not limited to the manufacturing sector. An investment management firm in the United Kingdom, Generation Investment Management, offers investment products that factor in the climate risks facing companies held in its portfolios. The insurance company AIG offers brokerage and greenhouse gas management services to clients participating in markets, such as the one operating in the European Union, for the buying and selling of greenhouse gas emissions allowances and credits.

Indeed, these new carbon markets create all kinds of opportunities for professional services firms, particularly financial institutions. Among other things, financial services firms can help companies craft the complex hedging and trading strategies needed to minimize costs in such markets.

Litigation Risk

Companies that generate significant carbon emissions face the threat of lawsuits similar to those common in the tobacco, pharmaceutical, and asbestos industries. For instance, in an unprecedented case spearheaded by the former New York attorney general Eliot Spitzer and currently being considered by the U.S. Second Circuit Court of Appeals, eight states and New York City have sued five of America's largest power companies, demanding that they cut carbon emissions. In a federal district court case in Mississippi, plaintiffs are suing oil and coal companies for greenhouse gas emissions, arguing that they contributed to the severity of Hurricane Katrina. The claims in that case include unjust enrichment, civil conspiracy (against the American Petroleum Institute), public and private nuisance, trespass, negligence, and fraudulent misrepresentation.

Companies that don't adequately address the issue of climate change also can create personal liabilities for directors and officers who become vulnerable to shareholder-related litigation. Swiss Re, for example, has found that such suits constitute a potential exposure in the company's directors and officers insurance portfolio.

Reputational Risk

Companies also face judgment in the court of public opinion, where they can be found guilty of selling or using products, processes, or practices that have a negative impact on the climate. The potential for consumer or shareholder backlash is particularly high in environmentally sensitive markets or in competitive sectors where brand loyalty is an important attribute of corporate value. In a recent study analyzing the impact of climate change on brand value, The Carbon Trust, an independent consultancy funded by the UK government, found that in some sectors the value of a company's brand could indeed be at risk because of negative perceptions related to climate change. As is the case in other risk areas, companies can turn reputational risk into an opportunity by leveraging practices that show them to be good citizens of the planet.

Physical Risk

Finally, there is the direct risk posed by the changing climate itself: physical effects such as droughts, floods, storms, and rising sea levels. The insurance, agriculture, fisheries, forestry, real estate, and tourism industries are particularly exposed because of their dependence on the physical environment and the elements. Physical climate risk can also affect sectors such as oil and gas through higher insurance premiums paid on assets located in vulnerable areas. Munich Re, for instance, raised its rates for insuring Gulf Coast oil rigs by 400% in the days after Hurricane Katrina struck. And ripples of physical risk can extend into some unexpected areas: For instance, Coca-Cola studies the linkages between climate change and water availability and how this will impact the location of its new bottling facilities.

Because companies' exposure to each of these six aspects of climate risk differs greatly, it is essential to generate tailored climate-risk profiles and strategies to mitigate the risk. Of course, companies in a given sector will have similar exposure to certain risks. For example, regulatory risks are more important in the power sector, while supply chain risks are critical in retail industries. But there also are differences within sectors—for example, varying levels of reputational risk.

It's important to remember that for some industries there is a direct upside to climate change, because government policy and public concern will create new needs and new markets. For instance, the "green buildings" market has historically occupied a tiny niche in the construction industry. Now, rising energy prices and resurgent public concern about sustainability have transformed the markets for environmentally friendly materials and technologies into explosive growth areas. The National Association of Homebuilders, for instance, estimates that green buildings will account for 5% to 10% of housing starts in 2010, up from 2% in 2005.

The venture capitalist John Doerr was recently quoted as saying that green technology could match information technology and biotechnology as a significant money-making opportunity. He called climate change "one of the most pressing global challenges" and said that the resulting demand for innovation would create the "mother of all markets."

Improving Your Company's Climate Competitiveness

In working with firms as they assess their exposure to climate change and begin to develop climate strategies, we have found that the most successful efforts include four key steps, each of which requires strong leadership at the top and involves significant learning across the organization.

Step 1: Quantify Your Carbon Footprint

Since you can manage only what you measure, companies need to first understand the source and level of their own greenhouse gas emissions and begin tracking those emissions over time. This quantitative and relatively straightforward task can lead to heightened consciousness of climate change issues within a company and set the stage for a broader look at the strategic risks and opportunities they pose.

In quantifying their carbon footprint, companies need to create an accurate inventory of their greenhouse gas emissions. They should differentiate between direct and indirect emissions—that is, between their own "smokestack" emissions and those resulting from their energy consumption, travel, and other activities. They should also establish and adjust emissions baselines and evaluate best practices in reporting this information. The aim is to identify and prioritize emission reduction opportunities and establish strategies for participating in greenhouse-gas-trading markets.

One method for performing this kind of accounting is the Greenhouse Gas Protocol, which our organization developed with the World Business Council for Sustainable Development. This tool, which has been taken up by the International Standards Organization, has been used by several hundred companies to measure and track their own greenhouse gas emissions and by industry groups, including the International Aluminum Institute and the International Council of Forest and Paper Associations, to develop complementary industry-specific calculation tools. (For a detailed explanation of how to use the protocol—along with a tool to help assess the value of emissions reduction initiatives and to factor climate-related costs into decisions on new capital projects—go to www.ghgprotocol.org.)

The pharmaceutical giant Pfizer has set guidelines requiring it to reduce its environmental footprint by lowering energy consumption. But that goal would be meaningless unless the company first created a systematic audit of its current activities that have a direct and indirect impact on greenhouse gas emissions. Having done that, the company can now identify possible conservation and emissions efficiency projects, which it reports through a companywide energy database. Pfizer has identified more than 600 such projects at all levels of the company.

Companies that quantify their footprints send a strong signal that they recognize the importance of climate change as a business risk—and an opportunity. We know of companies that began by conducting a carbon audit to uncover inefficient and costly energy practices and then moved on to identify opportunities for brand enhancement around the issue of climate change. As we'll see, these companies eventually leveraged their knowledge about climate-related issues to develop new and profitable products.

Step 2: Assess Your Carbon-Related Risks and Opportunities

The emissions footprint tells only part of the story. After determining the direct and indirect impact your company is having on the climate, you need to broaden your analysis and think strategically about how the six risks could hurt—or offer opportunities that better position—your business.

The forest products company Weyerhaeuser, whose mills create a significant carbon footprint, has committed to reducing operational emissions by 40% by 2020. But the company should also be considering climate-related issues beyond its emissions profile. Will the transportation costs to deliver its products rise significantly in a carbon-constrained economy? Are there potential physical effects of climate change on its main raw material, trees, such as greater damage by wood beetles because of milder winters?

Another way to assess the effect that climate-related forces will have on your company is to consider their direct and indirect financial impact. You can look at the "carbon intensity" of your profits—that is, what percentage is derived from products with high carbon dioxide emissions. Or you can look at ways in which climate change could affect your revenues and costs. On the cost side, climate change may drive increases in raw material costs, direct regulatory costs, capital expenditures (for example, new facilities with lower emissions levels), insurance premiums for assets located in at-risk areas (such as the Gulf Coast), and possibly even new tax liabilities. Revenues will be affected by your ability to pass these costs on to customers through new pricing structures while exploiting new market opportunities and maintaining market share. (See the sidebar "Climate Change and Profitability.")

The interplay among the various elements of climate-related risk affects a firm's cost of capital and ultimately its valuation. Investors will factor a company's climate exposure into estimates of its future cash flow streams. The degree to which cash flow is sensitive to climate risk will also affect how much cash is available for interest expense and amortization of a company's debt, ultimately affecting its ratings on bonds and bank debt.

Climate Change and Profitability

ONE WAY TO LOOK AT HOW climate-related forces will affect your company is to consider their impact on both costs and revenue. A company's ability to find opportunities in a carbon-constrained world will depend on its skill at hedging against physical climate risk, mitigating regulatory costs, avoiding expensive litigation and other threats to corporate reputation, managing climate risk in the supply chain, investing capital in low-carbon assets, and innovating around new technology and product opportunities.

Here are some prototype questions companies might ask themselves.

Potential Revenue Drivers

- How will changes in customer demand patterns affect pricing?

- What percentage of climate-related costs will we be able to pass through to customers?

- How can we generate streams of revenue from new low-carbon products?

Calculating the impact of climate risk on cash flows and costs of capital is critical to understanding your company's ability to compete in a carbon-constrained future.

Step 3: Adapt Your Business in Response to the Risks and Opportunities

Having assessed the ways in which climate change could affect your company, you will be prepared to develop strategies and make moves based on that knowledge. Those moves range from the obvious reductions in

- What new forms of income (for example, carbon credits) will become available?

- What threats do we face from low-carbon substitute products?

- What will be the impact of weather patterns on revenue?

Potential Cost Drivers

- How will regulatory policy affect our costs? (Will we need to purchase emissions allowances?)

- Is there a chance that emissions will also, or alternatively, be taxed?

- What capital expenditures do we face as a result of emissions-reduction plans?

- How much will our raw materials costs escalate? How much will those of our suppliers escalate?

- How much will our energy costs rise?

- How will our risk profile affect our insurance premiums?

energy consumption and carbon emissions to some-times wholesale reinventions of parts of your business.

Caterpillar is investing in making its already relatively low-emission diesel engines more efficient. It also has found opportunity in the risk of greater regulation by building a new business that makes particulate filter systems to be retrofitted on its own and others' engines. The company is studying turbines that run on alternative fuels, as well as combined heat and power generation turbines that recover waste heat. It is poised to commit significant R&D funds to these projects as soon as U.S. regulations put a cost on carbon emissions, thus making alternative fuels and technologies more attractive.

Creative moves aren't restricted to heavy manufacturing and other industries traditionally unfriendly to the environment. Wal-Mart is in the middle of a three-year plan to reduce energy use at its stores by up to 30%. The initiative, part of a highly publicized plan to boost energy efficiency, cut down on waste, and reduce greenhouse gas emissions, was launched not only to meet current or anticipated regulations but to burnish the company's reputation in an area where it had been attacked by critics.

In a lower-emissions sector, financial services, another industry in which reputation is important, Goldman Sachs has implemented a coordinated environmental-policy framework that, among other things, requires the measurement and reporting of greenhouse gas emissions attributable to its internal operations. The firm also is active in the burgeoning market for carbon allowances and has a team dedicated to doing research for clients on how environmental issues such as climate change can affect stock market valuations. The company's stated aim for these programs: to boost earnings.

"We're committing people, capital, and ideas to find effective market-based solutions to some of the most critical challenges facing the planet," Mark Tercek, the managing director of the Goldman Sachs Center for Environmental Markets, told us. "We see this as being entirely consistent with our central business objective of serving our clients and creating long-term value for our shareholders."

Step 4: Do It Better Than Your Competitors

If Tercek is to be proved right, though, a "doing well by doing good" approach won't be enough: You have to be better at it than your competitors. And that means beating them in both areas: reducing exposure to climate-related risks and finding business opportunities within those risks.

Take the auto industry, which we have studied in detail. Consumer concerns about national energy security, climate change, local air pollution, and the cost of filling up at the pump are shaping the competitive dynamics within the industry. In mapping the climate competitiveness of the major automakers three years ago, we looked at two things: how well they were positioned vis-à-vis climate risk and how they were managing climate opportunities. The analysis found that Honda and Toyota were best positioned to sell cars in a carbon-constrained economy, not only because their current fleets were more fuel efficient than most of their rivals' but also because they were leaders in the commercialization of hybrid vehicles. GM and Ford were burdened with above-average cost exposure because of the high proportion of fuel inefficient vehicles like SUVs and pickup trucks in their product lines. (Even among these gas-guzzlers, carbon emissions vary by as much as 40%, with the U.S. automakers' models being the least fuel efficient.) Detroit's failure to develop

Plotting Your Climate Competitiveness

REDUCING YOUR EXPOSURE to climate risk and creating new opportunities for profit are both important steps in building your climate competitiveness. But if your competitors are doing these things better, your company is losing ground.

In 2003, we mapped the climate competitiveness of the ten largest global automakers, looking at their vulnerability to risks and their ability to seize opportunities. Our analysis was conducted with Sustainable Asset Management, an investment management firm. Specifically, we evaluated the vulnerability of each automaker's current product line to further fuel-economy regulation by calculating the estimated cost per vehicle to meet new emissions standards during the following decade. We also analyzed how well the companies were managing climate opportunities. Using a zero-to-100 scale, we qualitatively assessed how advanced each automaker was in its ability to commercialize, market, and mass-produce vehicles using one or more low- carbon technologies—hybrid battery-and- gasoline, for example, or fuel-cell technology. Perhaps not surprisingly, we found that Honda and Toyota were best positioned to sell cars in a carbon-constrained economy, both because their current fleets were relatively fuel efficient and because they were ahead of rivals in commercializing new technologies.

---

innovative low-carbon technologies may be the greatest obstacle to their recovery. (For a look at how other automakers performed, using a matrix that could be applied to any industry, see the sidebar "Plotting Your Climate Competitiveness.")

General Electric has actively pursued competitive advantage through its climate policies. In 2003, it began using the Greenhouse Gas Protocol to construct an emissions inventory, allowing it to quantify its regulatory

To determine where your company stands with respect to your competitors, you can map your own industry using these two variables—positioning against risks and preparedness to seize opportunities. In doing so, you are likely to uncover ideas on how to move to a position of competitive advantage.

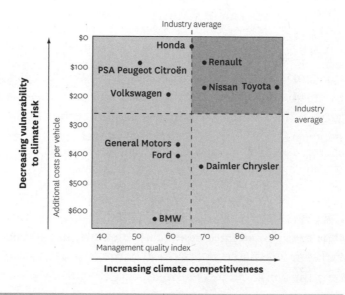

risk. It also joined a group of companies from different economic sectors—including Bristol-Myers Squibb, Citigroup, Con Edison, Johnson & Johnson, and Staples—to discuss climate strategies and learn from peers.

GE then began to think more strategically about how climate change could affect its business and that of its customers. In 2005, the company launched what it called Ecomagination, a coordinated product offering that features clean technologies that serve the transportation, energy, water, and consumer product sectors. GE's goals for the program were to double its annual investment in clean technologies to $1.5 billion by 2010 and to increase to at least $20 billion the revenue generated from products and services that offer customers measurable environmental performance advantages.

GE is already well on its way to reaching perhaps the most critical element of this strategy: increasing profits. Revenues from Ecomagination products reached $10.1 billion in 2005, with orders and commitments nearing $17 billion. And the R&D program is already paying off, with a 75% increase in certified Ecomagination products brought to market.

The aggressive moves by GE and other forward-looking companies show that climate change isn't a topic to repeatedly table until next year's meeting. It is already influencing the competitive dynamics in markets all over the world. As GE chairman and CEO Jeffrey Immelt recently commented, "Our customers have made it clear that providing solutions to environmental challenges like climate change is essential to society's well-being, and a clear growth opportunity for GE. Companies with the technology and vision to provide products and services that address climate and other pressing issues will enjoy a competitive advantage." Or, to put it differently, they will do not just well but *better* by doing good.

JONATHAN LASH is the president and FRED WELLINGTON is a senior financial analyst at the World Resources Institute, an environmental think tank based in Washington, DC.

Originally published in March 2007. Reprint R0703F

Index

You don't want to miss these...

We've combed through hundreds of *Harvard Business Review* articles on key management topics and selected *the* most important ones to help you maximize your own and your organization's performance.

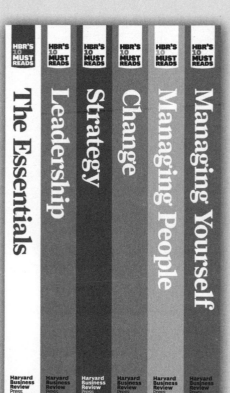